Surviving the 70's

By Benjamin DeMott

Surviving the 70's

Benjamin DeMott

E. P. DUTTON & CO., INC. | NEW YORK | 1971

Published simultaneously in Canada by Clarke, Irwin & Company
Limited, Toronto and Vancouver

Library of Congress Catalog Card Number: 75-146828

Grateful acknowledgment is given for permission to reprint the poem
"Well Water" by Randall Jarrell. Reprinted with permission of The Mac-
millan Company from *The Lost World* by Randall Jarrell. Copyright © by
Randall Jarrell, 1965.

The essays in this book appeared originally (under different titles or in
different form) in *The Atlantic, Change, Life, New American Review,* and
The New York Times.

SBN: 0-525-213104

To Theodore Baird

Contents

Foreword

For much of its length the book in your hand works at describing some new patterns of thought and feeling in contemporary culture. Hard to say a lot in a little about the patterns in question, but let me name a few assumptions that seem to count. People have come to believe that:

1. The character of human experience and human time can be altered: life is infinitely more pliant than our fathers knew.

2. The character of human experience and human time should be altered: present forms of experience (teaching, learning, loving, governing, worshiping, entertaining, child raising) are jails, barriers to flexibility, dehydrators of the human moment of being.

3. The wanted alterations will not take place merely through adjustment or liberalization of political or social opinion. Society must teach itself wholly new values, accept major new additions to its old declarations of blessedness, viz:

Blessed are those who interrupt, for practically everything now ongoing can profit from derailment or bad bumps.

Blessed is the sense of Possibility, for it is the prime energy-source of men who interrupt.

Blessed is Openness (open personalities, open classrooms, openness to experience in the large), for it alone protects interrupters from falling into habit and passivity of their own.

From assumptions like these, many human and social problems inevitably flow. The great god Possibility encourages men to be fantasts, forgetful of the responsibilities that begin in probabilities rather than in dreams, forgetful too of the human need for markers, maps, sightlines, balancing points, cherished solidities of terrain, as well as for fresh pastures new. No less inevitably, the new assumptions, and the emergent sensibility they're shaping, create big opportunities—a chance of ending social and moral compartmentalization, moving toward fuller development of the human capacity to constructively imagine, and care about, lives different from one's own. The aim of thinking and writing about all this—I admit it sounds dull and teacherly—the aim in "understanding" it, is to teach yourself how to be adequate to both the problems and the opportunities. Only alertness to the mixed character of experience in revolutionary times can point a way to dry ground, when tides of mad euphoria, despair or apocalypse begin to rise.

As would be guessed, the assessments and understandings arrived at in this book are personal, and the recurring questions are homely: how much New Thought can actually go down in a stable middle life? How can a human being (as opposed to History in the large) cope, in his own local, limited head, with the tilts of assumption and belief now occurring regularly in all corners of the culture? Your children are polite but detached about jobs and marriages, yours included; your young employee promotes herself to full partnership overnight; your neighbor's wife goes fiercely women's lib; the first-rate novelist in your hand says, Quit, civilization is finished; your friend and former student, fifteen years out, berates you in print for not being a Maoist in 1955; your college's top science graduate, cropped, scrubbed, confident, informs you commune life is absolutely the only thing; you wake up on the morning of a new decade resolved to explain to yourself as clearly as you can what exactly happened during the ten-year night before and you can't say a word. . . . What then follows? What sequences of thought and feeling shape a man's innerness in such circumstances? What kinds of order can a mind work out for itself? Answering such questions is the writer's work, at least as it shows itself here.

But it won't do to imply that at every moment the present writer stands in the same relation to his materials. A good deal of what follows, whether about commune intellection or ecological rhetoric or the decline of the ratrace, was written at something like a calm remove from the "revolutionary" phenomena under analysis. And, as has often been demonstrated, it's one thing to speak of these phenomena when you feel yourself to be in charge—shaping your argument, marshaling evidence, etc.— and another to know an interruption from inside. The campus strike journal at the end of this book testifies that losing your way is easy, that no amount of chat about "cultural revolution" prepares you for your own moment of experiential surprise, that even the mildest eruption, genteel, unbloody, raises a question whether survival can be brought off without a descent into self-glorification or politomania.

Reading over these sentences I see that the part above about a mind working out order on its own implies solitariness, independence, originality, etc. Trash that, as children say. Scouting around for a personal perspective, something more than "correct" descriptive labels, means leaning hard on other minds—scores of them, including many that aren't household words. A practiced leaner, I try to name the leaned-ons as I go. But such acknowledgments, name by name, don't in themselves say enough about the psychological (as opposed to intellectual) benefits of leaning. The case is that it's the example of the community of "other minds," unselfish clarifiers, flexy heads, men of hope, relishers who've stayed at it, hunting down contemporary strengths and weaknesses—it's that example that gives the sharpest sense of what a genuine, non-crisis-ridden possibility-culture would feel like. Study that community and you glimpse the open future here in the present, even as you pick up, if not the secret of running unity through a book, truth about how and why to go on going on.

August 16, 1970
Amherst, Mass.

I

Thinking Now

The Way It Is:
Some Notes on What We Feel

Hard times, confusing times. All at once—no warnings or trendy winks from the past—we've become New People, putting demands to ourselves and to life in the large for which precedents don't exist. And because the scale of our transformation causes inward ruptures, harries us into feelings and expectations that have no names, our nerves are shaky, we shuttle between nostalgia and a manic optimism—behave always as though out at some edge.

If we grasped our situation, had a clear concept of where we were and why, we might suffer less. But where can we turn for clarification? Among a thousand wonders, the period is remarkable for the absence of a fully humane genius among those who represent us to ourselves. Vast step-ups of production schedules have occurred in the art-and-culture-commentary industries, and substantial talents breathe among us, pump hard, fight for and win wide audiences. Yet no image or vocabulary adequate to the truth of the age comes forth. The need is for perspective and comparative evalution, acts of consideration and assessment, and we've been offered instead—the notion of "blame" is irrelevant: the work produced probably could not have been otherwise, given the time—discrete patches of intensity, special pleading and description, and virtually no interpretation worth the name.

Wife-swapping (John Updike), protest marches (Norman Mailer), exotic theatrical and cinematic entertainments (Susan Sontag), acid-tripping and radical chic (Tom Wolfe)—these and a hundred other "characteristic phenomena" are evoked in exacting, often exciting detail and with superlative attentiveness to personal response. But the place of the phenomena in moral history, the interrelationships among them, the chief forces and principles determining the nature of the emergent new sensibility, are left undefined. Often, in fact, the pitchman's cant and jargon—copywriters' tags like *The Scene . . . getting it all together . . . encounter group . . . enter the dialogue . . . a piece of the action . . . with it . . . Now generation*—appear to contain better hints to our truth than does any novel, essay or play.

And from this failure of art and intellect to nourish and illuminate, many problems flow. One is our readiness to accept "explanations" of ourselves that actually deepen the general confusion. There is, for instance, the hugely popular delusion that the central development of our time has been the widening of the gap between youth and everybody else. The yearly periodical indices disclose that three to four times as many words are now being written about youth as were written a decade ago. And the statistic reflects the growth of a superstition that the story of the age may simply be the simultaneous appearance of two ages, two worlds—one belonging to young people and the other to the rest of us—and that the prime influence on behavior and feeling in both worlds is the attitude of each toward the other.

A handy formula: it provides a means of organizing events, tastes, gestures. But if the order thus established is convenient, it's also primitive: you buy it only at the cost of blindness to the essential unity of the period. The college senior demanding the "restructuring" of his commencement ceremonies, the company president struggling to "involve" minor line executives in top-echelon decisions, the guerrilla-theater propagandist sneering at old-style radicals for being "hung up on words and argufying"—these clearly aren't the same man. Yet ignoring the connections among their apparently disparate behaviors, pretending that the task of cultural inquiry amounts to finding out "what the young are thinking," as though the latter lived not among us but on remote, inaccessible islands, is a mistake. This is an age; what's happened, baby, has happened to men as well as babes; we can indeed say "we," and the sniffish fear of doing so continues to cost us to this day.

One other expensive delusion demands notice—namely, the view that our newness is a function of an unexampled fury of sensation-hunting. Easy to adduce evidence supporting this theory, to be sure. Contemporary man has been a tripper in many senses; recent years saw incredible expansions of air travel, motel chains, tourist agencies. The manufacture, on demand, of variety goes on without pause—*Hair, Che, Dionysus, Commune,* Breslin, Millett, Reich, Barbados, Eleuthera, the Algarve, Arthur, Electric Circus, Max's Plum, Beatles, Doors, Led Zeppelin, topless, bottomless, bare. . . . And it's undeniable that the age has created vehicles and instruments of sensation on an order of arousal power never before legitimized by the consent of an entire society. But we nevertheless simplify ourselves, enshroud our lives in a mist of moralizing, if we accept as an adequate perspective what in fact is no more than a style of self-laceration. We are not, in the broad mass, pure sensationalists, snappers-up of unconsidered kicks; without denying the chaos and the extravagance, it can still be claimed that the age has more dignity, promise and intellectual complication than any such formula allows.

Wherein lies the complication? If we aren't out for sensation alone, what are we after? Where is our center, what are our growing points, what actually has been happening in our lives?

Best to answer flatly: major changes have been occurring in our sense of self, time and dailiness. For one thing, we've become obsessed with Experience. (We behave, that is to say, as though we're determined to change our relation to our experience, or to have our "usual" experiences in new ways.) For another, we've come to relish plurality of self. (We behave as though impatient or bitter at every structure, form, convention and practice that edges us toward singleness of view or "option," or that forces us to accept this or that single role as the whole truth of our being.) For yet another, we seem to be striving to feel time itself on different terms from those hitherto customary. (We're anxious to shed ordinary, linear, before-and-after, cause-and-effect under-standings of events even in our personal lives. We feel distaste for inward response that's insufficiently alive to The Moment, or that glides over each instant as a betweenness—in another minute it'll be time to go to work, go to dinner, write our brother, make love, do the dishes—rather than living into it, inhabiting it as an occasion, without thought of antecedents or consequences.) And finally, we've conceived a detestation of the habitual. (We are seeking ways of opening our minds and characters to the multi-plicity of situations that are echoed or touched or alluded to by any one given situation. We hope to replace habit—"the shackles of the free," in Bierce's great definition—with a continually re-newed alertness to possibility.)

As goes without saying, labeling and categorizing in this manner is presumptuous: the congeries of inexpressible attitudes and assumptions in question is dense, intricate, tightly packed—more so than any confident arbitrary listing can suggest. And, as also should go without saying, the vocabulary used here to name the assumptions isn't much favored by any of us who're just "get-ting through the days" called the seventies. We don't tell our-selves, "We must change our relation to our experience." We don't say, "I must find a new way of having my experience." We live by no abstract formulas, we simply express our preferences. We perhaps say, in planning a political meeting: "Let's not have so many speeches this time." We perhaps say, when serving on a parish committee to reinvigorate a WASP church: "Let's have a different kind of service at least once. . . . Once a month, maybe." We perhaps say at conferences: "When do we break into small groups?" We perhaps say, if we're a girl and boy preparing for a costume party (a girl in a midi did in fact say, Halloween night, at Hastings Stationery in Amherst, Massachusetts, over by the greeting cards, to her date), "Look, why don't we just change clothes? I'll go in your stuff, you wear my midi." And it's clearly a jump from innocuous jokes of this sort to the solemn apparatus of historical statement.

On occasion, though, we ourselves do grow more explicit or

theoretical. Certain exceptional situations—or community pressures—have drawn from some of us flat declarations that our aim is to change our relation to our experience. Middle-class drug users do say aloud, for example, that they use drugs, pot or acid, in order to create simultaneously a wholly new sense of personal possibility, and to alter the inner landscape of time so that experience can be occupied, known in its own moment-to-moment quality, texture, delight, rather than as a backdrop for plans, intentions, anxieties. And if the majority is vastly less explicit than this about its intentions, if the unity of our purposes escapes most of us, we nevertheless do venture forth, time and time over, old, young, middle-aged, in situations of striking range, and do the thing itself—arrange, that is, to have our experience in new ways.

Some of our contrivances are mainly amusing—fit matter for *New Yorker* cartoons. They take the form of homely efforts at energizing recreation or casual relations with others, or at injecting the values of surprise—or even of moderated risk—into commonplace situations. The long-hair fad, feminization of costume and behavior, cosmetics for men, Unisex, etc.: here is an attempt to create a new way of having the experience of masculinity (or femininity). If freedom is most real when most on trial, then masculinity will be most piquantly masculine when set in closer adjacency to its "opposite": let me have my sexuality as conscious choice rather than as taken-for-granted, unopposable, unconfrontable bio-cultural conditioning. Or again: the taste of the sons and daughters of the middle class for tattered clothes, worn jeans, torn shoes, soul music, coarse language, rucksacks, thumbing—or for stripping to bare skin, as at Woodstock—is expressive of a yearning to have the experience of middle-class life in a fresh way, with an allusion to the life of the field hand or the workingman or the savage, and with a possibility vivid at every moment, at least in one's own fantasy, of being taken for something that (by objective definition) one isn't.

And there are countless comparable efforts—tentative, self-conscious, touching and hilarious by turns—to transform or ventilate familiar patterns of experience. The intimidated young grow beards and find a new way to have the experience of intimidation—as intimidators rather than as the intimidated. Men slightly older, stockbrokers or editors, grow beards and live for a moment, in a passing glance met on the street or subway, as figures momentarily promoted to eccentricity, individuality, mystery. The fashionably decorous find a new way of combining the experience of being fashionable with that of displaying sexual fury and abandon—The Scene, the pounding, raging discotheque. The experience of the theatergoer and moviegoer is complicated and "opened to possibility" by the invention of participatory theater and the art-sex film. (The routine moviegoing experience occurs in a new way at sex documentaries because of nervous consciousness among patrons of their adjacency to each other; the experience of theatergoing occurs in a new way at *Hair* or La Mama or the Living Theater or the Performance Group because of nervous consciousness among the audience of its relations with the players.) Even the most ordinary activities—driving a car—are touched by the energizing spirit. And here as elsewhere risks are offered at a variety of levels. The timid can participate, while motoring, in the decal dialogue—flags vs. flowers, hardhats vs. hippies, on windshields and hoods. (The politicization of tourism.) The more daring can affix risqué bumper stickers and thereby possess an idea of themselves not merely as traveling or politicking but as, at any given moment, escalating to Don Juanism.

Predictably, the influence of the new impulses and assumptions has produced—even among "safe" middle-class people—behavior that's empty, ugly or pathetic: frivolous sexual indulgence, promiscuity, group sexual "experiments," attempts to restore lyric quality to humdrum domesticity by the gaudy device of The Affair. And predictably the influence of the new taste is easiest to read in the exotic trades and professions. The intellectual journalist seeks to change his relation to his work by crossing his objective function as a noter of external events with an enterprise in self-analysis—scrutiny of the unique intricacies of his own response to the occurrences "covered." Painters and sculptors for their part aim at altering their own and their audience's experience as gallery-goers by impacting that experience with the experience of the supermarket or with that of the toyshop or hobbyist's tool table. Directors like Julian Beck and Richard Schechner show actors how to alter the terms of their experience: no longer need the actor imitate another person, play a "role," learn a part.

He can simultaneously act and be: by presenting his own nature, using his own language, setting forth his own feelings in a dynamic with an audience, establishing relations in accordance with momentary shifts of personal feeling, and thereby foreclosing no possibility within himself. And similar opportunities stem from the new terms of relatedness between performers and audience throughout the worlds of showbiz and sports—witness the example of the surprising intimacies of the new sports heroes or a dozen rock stars with their fans.

But it's not only in exotic worlds of work or leisure that men labor to invent new ways of having familiar experience. That effort has touched American culture in scores of unlikely places, from the condominium and the conglomerate to priestly orders and women's liberation cells and books by George Plimpton. And because the "movement," to speak of it as that, is universal, the economic consequences are overwhelming. The desire to combine plain locomotion with adventure, "engagement with reality," recreated the family wagon as Mustang or Camaro and sold 10 million sports cars. Corporations able to manufacture, for people immured in seemingly unchangeable situations, a means of moving toward an alternative experience, expand immensely—witness the growth of Avon Products, which sells the possibility of Fatal Womanhood to housewives unable to "get out." Everywhere the consumer pursues the means and images of another life, a different time, a strange new window on experience. And the supplier's ingenuity is breathtaking, as attested by Tom Wolfe's account of the marketing of militancy among the rich, or his inventory of the contents of the novelist Ken Kesey's "house":

"Day-Glo paint . . . Scandinavian-style blonde . . . huge floppy red hats . . . granny glasses . . . sculpture of a hanged man . . . Thunderbird, a great Thor-and-Wotan beaked monster . . . A Kama Sutra sculpture . . . color film . . . tape recorders . . ."

The range of materials manufactured in this country to meet the demand for self-transformation and extension of role has become so extraordinary, indeed, that a wholly new kind of mail-order catalogue has lately begun to appear. One such—the 128-page *Whole Earth Catalogue* (1969-71)—lists thousands of commercially produced products of use to ordinary men bent on moving beyond the limits of their training, job or profession in order to participate (by their own effort) in the life styles of others—farmers, geologists, foresters, you name it.

None of this would matter greatly, of course—much of it would seem eligible for only satiric regard—if it could be neatly separated from the major political events of recent years. But as is often true of alterations of sensibility, the new feeling for "possibility" and the new dream of plural selves can't be thus separated. Throughout the sixties these forces had measureless impact on public as well as upon private life, and their influence has lately been intensified.

To speak of the influence with appropriate balance is difficult: political acts have political content—indefensible to propose some latter-day version of the old-style Freudian "medical egotism" which substituted chatter about neuroses and psychoses for political explanations of the course of national affairs. For that reason it needs to be said aloud once more—about, say, the teachers and students who participated in the first teach-ins against the Vietnam war in 1964 and '65, or in the strike against the Cambodian invasion in 1970, ventures whose consequences for men and nations still can't be fully accounted—that these were not trivial men acting out quirkish desires to escape into the Enveloping Scene, or into The Unpredictable. They were passionately concerned to alter what they regarded as a senseless, perilous, immoral course of adventurism.

But true as this is, the current behavior of teachers and students does have psychocultural as well as political ramifications. The "politically concerned" member of an American faculty knew in former days what his prescribed role was: to observe, to make amusing remarks. He might examine (ironically, in asides) the substance of his frustration or impotence—shrug it off in a glancing commentary in his classes, nothing more. During the teach-ins and in the earlier Cuban crisis, he and many of his students stepped beyond these limits, reached out toward another self. No longer a teacher in the orthodox form, nevertheless he still taught; no longer a disseminator or accumulator of knowledge in the conventional frame, he still pursued understanding. He passed through the conventional frame with his students, advanced from the warehouse of reported experience—graphs, charts, texts—and appeared now as a grappler with immediacy, a man bidding for influence in the shaping of public policy even in the act of teaching, laboring to possess the teacher's experience in a new way.

And precisely this determination figured at the center of the major political event of this age. It is the black man's declaration of his sense of possibility that, more than any other single force, is shaping these years. Whipped, lynched, scourged, mocked, prisoned in hunger, his children bombed, his hope despised, the American black was the archetypal "limited self": no movement feasible, seemingly, save from despair to a junkie's high. The glory and terror of our age is the awakened appetite for new selfhood, new understandings of time, new ground for believing in the pliancy of experience, on the part of 20 million black Americans. Their grasp of the meaning of "open" experience lends a color of dignity even to the most trivial venture in self-extension elsewhere in the culture. And nothing is more striking than that they truly are demanding multiplicity, will not trade off blackness for whiteness, will not substitute one simplicity for another. The aim is to add a new self and participate in a new life with no sacrifice of the old.

Everywhere in the culture, in sum, the same themes sound: the will to possess one's experience rather than be possessed by it, the longing to live one's own life rather than be lived by it, the drive for a more various selfhood than men have known before. Few efforts to summarize those themes convey the energy, excitement and intensity of the longing. ("There is an increased demand by all parts of the citizenry," says the Teachers College Center for Research and Education in American Liberties, in mild voice, "for participation in decision-making in all areas of public and private institutional life.") Few men can contemplate the new demands without contradictory responses, fear and trembling among them. But whatever the response, the unity of sensibility lies beyond denial. Young, old, black, white, rich and poor are pursuing the dream of a more vital experience. Propelled often by the belief that if we know the good, then we must act the good, we're moving from passive to active, from "package to prove." And at the root of our yearning stand the twin convictions: that we can be more, as men, than we're permitted to be by the rule of role and profession, and that the life of dailiness and habit, the life that lives us, precedes us, directs us to the point of suppressing moral conscience and imagination, is in truth no life at all.

Fine, fine, says a voice: it's a way of describing a cultural change. But why the change in the first place? All that mid-century agonizing about Conformity, Silent Generation, etc. And then this sudden outbreak, this demand (if you will) for more life, more selves, the open sense of time and the rest: how and why is it happening? Surely not a simple cyclical process . . .

For philosophers of the media the question holds no mysteries. Nothing more natural, they consider, than for people to ask more of themselves now: men are more, as men, than they used to be. Through the centuries we've been extending ourselves steadily, touching and comprehending life at ever-greater distances from our immediate physical environment. Lately we press a button and a world of hot events pours into our consciousness —at peace we know war; in the clean suburb we know the blighted ghetto; sober and rational we watch doomed men turn on; law-abiding and confident, we watch the furtive cop collect his grease. As we hold the paper in our hands we know that somewhere on earth an excitement yet undreamed is tracked for us: hijackers whirled across the sky are tied to us with umbilical cables. And the knowledge quickens our belief in a fascinating otherness that could be, that will be, momentarily ours. Why would we rest content in mere is-ness? What can our experience be but a ceaseless prodding by the demons of Possibility?

Nor do the philosophers stop here. Marshall McLuhan argues that, because of its low-definition picture, TV has restructured the human mind, remade mental interiors in the Kantian sense, creating new aptitudes, new schema of perception, which in turn foster generalized enthusiasm for "involvement and participation" throughout the culture. . . . "TV has affected the totality of our lives, personal and social and political," he writes. "If the medium is of high definition, participation is low. If the medium is of low intensity, the participation is high. . . . In 10 years the new tastes of America in clothes, in food, in housing, in entertainment and in vehicles [will] express the new pattern of . . . do-it-yourself involvement fostered by the TV image."

A match for the ingenuity of this sort of explanation is found in the writings of some who propose existential philosophy as a Key Influence on the age. Since the philosophy asserts the precedence of the person over the culturally fixed function or situation (so runs the argument), and since its themes are well diffused, is it not reasonable to feel its presence in the new insistence on a man's right to break free of the constraints of special social or professional roles?

Perhaps—but the likelihood is strong in any case that the engulfing public events of recent years have had a shade more to do with our new attitudes and psychology than the line count in the boob tube or the essays of Merleau-Ponty. A powerful lesson taught by the Vietnam war from the mid-sixties onward, for example, was that bureaucrats, diplomats, generals and presidents who allow themselves to be locked into orthodox, culturally-sanctioned patterns of thought and assumption make fearful mistakes. Men came to believe that it was because General Westmoreland was a general, a military man to the core, that he could not admit to scrutiny evidence that challenged his professional competency. No event in American history cast sterner doubt on the efficacy of the limited professional self—on the usefulness of clear-eyed, patent-haired, inhumanly efficient defense secretaries, technicians, worshipers of military "intelligence"—than the disasters that followed every official optimistic pronouncement about Vietnam from the middle sixties onward.

Because men of authority were inflexible, locked into Chief-Executivehood, because they couldn't bring themselves to believe in the upsurges of The Scene that destroy careful, sequential, cause-and-effect narratives, human beings by the tens of thousands were brutally slaughtered. What good therefore was the perfected proficiency that took a man to the top? We had begun learning, in the fifties, to say the phrase "The Establishment" in a tone of contempt. In those early days the chief target was a certain self-protectiveness, caution—and snootiness—in the well placed. But the war showed The Establishment forth as a particular style of intellectual blindness and emotional rigidity: those black suits, high-rise collars, unctuous assurances, fabled undergraduate distinctions at Harvard and Yale, 19-hour days, those in-group back-patting sessions, at length came to appear, in the eyes of people at every level of life, as a kind of guarantee of self-loving self-deception. Lead us not into that temptation, so went the general prayer: give us back our flexibility.

And the prayer for variousness, for a way out of "structured experience," has been hugely intensified by the national traumas through which we've passed. In the moments of national shame and grief and terror—the killing of the Kennedys, of Martin Luther King, Malcolm X—a new truth came belatedly but fiercely home. Our fixities weren't objectionable simply because they were fixities: they carried within them, unbeknown to the generations that kept faith with them, a charge of human unconcern and viciousness that positively required a disavowal of the past—flat rejection of past claims to value, principle or honor. For the seed of our traumas, whether assassinations or riots, seemed invariably to lie in racism, in a willful determination to treat millions of human beings as less than human. The contemplation of the deaths of heroes, in short, opened a door for us on our own self-deceit and on the self-deception practiced by our fathers. Neither they nor we had told it like it was. And they were apparently all unaware that because of their fantasies and obliviousness millions suffered. They spoke of goodness, of social and family values, of man's responsibility to man, they spoke of community, fidelity, ethics, honor before God, and never obliged themselves to glance at the gap between their proclamations and the actualities their uncaringness created. Their way of inhabiting doctor-dom, law-yer-dom, sober citizenhood, their ways of having the experience of respectable men, shut them in a prison of self-love and unob-servance: who among us could bear so airless, priggish, mean a chamber?

Had we had no help in ascertaining the relevant facts, had the discoverers and representatives of the Black Experience not writ-ten their books, we might have been slower to ask such questions. Dr. King's dream might have moved us less, and lived less vividly in memory, had James Baldwin not written *The Fire Next Time,* or had there been no successors—no Cleaver, no LeRoi Jones— or had we been unprepared by the earlier struggles, marches and rides.

But what matters here is that the discovery of the Black Ex-perience has filled us with a sense that, if we are connected with the history that shaped that experience, then the connection should be broken. Let us no longer dress or act or feel as our predecessors had done, let us no longer be educated passively in lies as we had been, let us no longer listen politely to the "authorities" sanctimoniously assuring us that history is "important" or that the great writers "must be mastered" or that truth is tradition or that virtue equals a stable self. Our obligation to the past, the credibility of those who spoke of the dignity of the departed— blind men, crude unbelievers in the human spirit—these are vanishing, leaving us freer of the hand of the past than any before us have been. Faith of our fathers—what God could sponsor that faith? How can we be men and go on living in the old ways in the old house?

And then over and beyond all this, though entangled with it in subtle potent ways, there has arisen an unprecedented outcry against human dailiness itself. The outcry I speak of isn't rationalized as an onslaught against moral obliviousness. It appears also to be beyond politics, domestic or foreign, and without philosophical content. Its single thrust is the claim that middle-class life is unredeemable not by virtue of its being evil but because it is beyond measure boring.

Consider recent literary patterns. The last decade opened with pronouncements by Norman Mailer against the dreariness of safe, habitual life and for violence and brutality, even when practiced by mindless teen-agers murdering a helpless old man, as an escape from deadly dailiness. A few years later, a chorus of sick comics and "black-humor" novelists were being applauded for social commentary issuing directly from professed disgust with every aspect of habit-ridden middle-class life.

And, arguably more important, whenever middle-class experience was represented at any length and with any care in our period, the artist obdurately refused to include a detail of feeling that would hint at imaginative satisfactions—or openings of possibility—feasible within the middle life. Teaching a toddler to swim, for instance—a familiar cycle. Coaxed and reassured, my child at length jumps in laughing from poolside, absolute in trust of my arms; a second later she discovers that by doing my bidding she can "stay up," move; watching in delight, I'm touched and freshened. I see I'm trusted and worth trusting, emulated and worth emulating. . . . What a drag, says mod fiction, what senti-

mentality, how trivial. . . . In the domestic pages of John Updike's *Couples,* no mother is radiated by the beauty of her child
bathing in the tub. No father learns, with a lift of pride, of his
son's meeting a hard responsibility well and tactfully. The insistence on boredom, weariness, repetitiveness, burdensomeness
is unrelenting; crankiness, leftovers, nagging, falsity, insufferable
predictability—these are presented as the norms of the workaday-
weekend cycle. Grown men join together for a recreational game
of basketball in Mr. Updike's novel—but, although the author is
superb at rendering sensation, he creates no pleasure of athletic
physicality, nor even the act of slaking decent thirst. Everywhere
his talk assures the reader There Must Be More Than This, nowhere in the texture of dailiness can he find a sudden, sweet in-
crement of surprise, a scene that permits "modest, slow, molecular, definitive, social work," or any other hope for renewal:

> Foxy . . . was to experience this sadness many times, this chronic
> sadness of late Sunday afternoon, when the couples had ex-
> hausted their game, basketball or beachgoing or tennis or touch
> football, and saw an evening weighing upon them, an evening
> without a game, an evening spent among flickering lamps and
> cranky children and leftover food and the nagging half-read
> newspaper with its weary portents and atrocities, an evening
> when marriages closed in upon themselves, like flowers from
> which the sun is withdrawn, an evening giving like a smeared
> window on Monday and the long week when they must perform
> again their impersonations of working men, of stockbrokers and
> dentists and engineers, of mothers and housekeepers, of adults
> who are not the world's guests but its hosts.

Whether writers of this commitment and assumption are
creators of the age less than they are its victims can't be known.
Whether their voices would have sufficed to persuade us of the
uselessness of sequential, predictable, "closed-self" ways of having our experience, had there been no war and no black rebellion,
we can't be certain. It's clear, though, that a man who seeks in
the popular literature of this age, an image of his life that allows
for possibility and freshening within the context of dailiness, and
without loss of stable selfhood, isn't able to find it: in our world,
so says the official dictum, it's quite impossible to breathe.

But, says another voice, is it impossible? Or, asking the question in a different way, can we truly survive if we persist in our

present direction? Suppose we continue on our present course, pressing for new selves and new ways of experiencing. Will we be nourishing a growing point for humanness? Can a humane culture rise on any such foundations?

For pessimists several reminders are pertinent. One is that the taste for Immediate Experience and Flexible Selves is deeply in the American grain. The belief in the power of unmediated experience to show men where they err—and how to cope—was powerful on the American frontier, and survives in the writings of virtually every major American thinker in our past. Again and again in the pages of Thoreau, Emerson, William James, Peirce and Dewey "pure" Experience is invoked as teacher, and again and again these sages set forth a demand for Openness. Habit, routinized life, fixed manners, conventions, customs, the "usual daily round"—these block us off from knowledge and also from concern for the lives of those different from ourselves. Therefore (our native sages concluded) therefore, shake free of the deadening job or ritual, escape into the grace of wholeness, fly in the direction of surprise and the unknown—in that direction lie the true beginnings of a man.

And there is far more to the return to the ideal of open experience than the ineluctable American-ness of the thing. The return is itself a symbol of an awakened awareness of the limits of reason and of the danger that constant interventions of intellect between ourselves and experience hide from us the truth of our natural being, our deep connectedness with the natural world that the technological mind has been poisoning. And, more important than any of this—for reasons already named—there is a moral and spiritual content to the rejection of the structures of the past which, though now increasingly deprecated, has unshakable vigor and worth.

There are, however, immense problems. The immediate-experience, multiple-selves cause contains within it an antinomian, anti-intellectual ferocity that has thus far created fears chiefly about the safety of institutions—universities, high schools, legislatures, churches, political conventions. But the serious cause for alarm is the future of mind. The love of the Enveloping Scene as opposed to orderly plodding narratives, fondness for variety of self rather than for stability, puts the very idea of mind under extraordinary strain. It is, after all, by an act of sequential reasoning that Norman O. Brown and many another characteristic voice of our time arrived at their critique of the limits of consecutive thought. Once inside the scene, utterly without a fixed self, will our power to compare, assess and choose survive?

Within the past few years men have begun thinking purposefully on these problems, aware that "planning" would necessarily henceforth be in bad odor, yet unconvinced that the future could be met with any hope whatever minus the resources of intellect. One question addressed was: Can society be reorganized in a manner that will accommodate the appetite for self-variousness and possibility—without insuring the onset of social chaos? (Among the most brilliant suggestions were those advanced by Professors Donald Oliver and Fred Newmann in a *Harvard Education Review* paper [1967] that looked toward the invention of a world in which men may move freely at any point in their postpubescent lives into and away from the roles of student, apprentice and professional.) Another question addressed was: Can society be so organized as to permit genuine simultaneities of role? Is it possible to create situations in which we can simultaneously engage our resources as domestic man, political man, inquiring man? (The most imaginative effort in this direction now in progress is a two-year-old Office of Education venture in educational reform—Triple T, Training of Teacher-Trainers. The scheme has enlisted scholars, professional instructors in pedagogy and a significant segment of laymen and minority group representatives—barbers to bankers—in cooperative planning and carrying out of experimental teaching programs in dozens of local communities around the nation.)

These are small beginnings—but already some significant truths have appeared. It is clear that men on the conservative side, "defenders of orthodox values" (professional, social or academic), need to be disabused of the wishful notion that heroic, do-or-die Last Stands for tradition are still feasible. The movement of culture—what's happening—has happened so irreversibly, the changes of assumption and of cultural texture are so thoroughgoing, that the idea of drawing a line—thus far and no farther—is at best comic. The option of Standing Pat has been foreclosed; there is no interest on the part of the "opposition" in face-to-face struggle; when and if traditionalists march forth to an imagined Fateful Encounter, they'll find only ghosts and shadows waiting.

And on the radical side, it's clear that the task is somehow to establish that the reason for rehabilitating the idea of the stable self, and the narrative as opposed to the dramatic sense of life, is to insure the survival of the human capacity to have an experience. For as John Dewey put it years ago:

> Experiencing like breathing is a rhythm of intakings and outgivings. Their succession is punctuated and made a rhythm by the existence of intervals, periods in which one phase is ceasing and the other is inchoate and preparing. [We compare] the course of a conscious experience to the alternate flights and perchings of a bird. The flights are intimately connected with one another; they are not so many unrelated lightings succeeded by a number of equally unrelated hoppings. Each resting place in experience is an undergoing in which is absorbed and taken home the consequences of prior doing, and, unless the doing is that of utter caprice or sheer routine, each doing carries in itself meaning that has been extracted and conserved. . . . If we move too rapidly, we get away from the base of supplies—of accrued meanings—and the experience is flustered, thin and confused. If we dawdle too long after having extracted a net value, experience perishes of inanition.

Despite the cultural revolution, we possessed until very recently, a poet of "perchings," a believer in human rhythms who was capable of shrewd distinctions between caprice and routine, and firm in his feeling for the ordinary universe—and for the forms of ordinary human connectedness. Randall Jarrell (1914–1965) could write of ordinary life that it was a matter of errands generating each other, often a tiresome small round, the pumping of a rusty pump, water seeming never to want to rise—and he could then add that within the round, to alert heads, came a chance to act and perceive and receive, to arrive at an intensity of imaginative experience that itself constitutes an overflowing and a deep release:

> . . . sometimes
> The wheel turns of its own
>   weight, the rusty
> Pump pumps over your
>   sweating face the clear

Water, cold, so cold! You cup
your hands
And gulp from them the
dailiness of life.

The shadow over us just now is that we seem too disposed to disbelieve in that nourishment—almost convinced it can't be real. But we nevertheless possess some strength, a possible way forward. We know that within the habitual life are a thousand restraints upon feeling, concern, humanness itself: our growing point is that we have dared to think of casting them off.

In and Out of Women's Lib

Hear out a contemporary domestic story: uncommon yesterday, tomorrow (possibly) a norm. The theme is the subtilization of a marriage. The action, as befits domestic tales, is undramatic—a matter of shifts of inward understanding of self and family that alter the quality of one couple's shared life. As for the characters—

Call them Robert and Eloise, picturing (as you do) an academic male, decent, ectomorphic, and (as Eloise) a round-faced, comely woman with a hint of the quality—unillusioned humorous intelligence?—and a lot of the looks of the Comtesse Daru in the Frick Gallery's David portrait. Mid-thirtyish, parents of three, this couple makes its home on the campus of a well-heeled Maryland boarding school where Robert works as assistant head and senior history master. Change entered their lives two years ago, when the couple decided Eloise (a Smith graduate) should finish the required education courses and begin a school career. (The idea was Robert's; it occurred to him after Eloise took on

the school farmer's allegedly "slow" twin boys in math and
French—friendly gesture—and watched them soar from hopeless
"Phase 2" to college-bound "Phase 4.") The decision wasn't lightly
arrived at, even though the usual problems—sitter, transporta-
tion, etc.—were in this instance easily met. The obstacle was
Eloise. She thought (a) that there was an element of faddish-
ness in Moms racing back to the labor market; (b) that amid a
pack of undergraduates in a strange university she might begin
feeling old and why did she need that? (c) that it was pleasant
to read and think what she wanted, instead of being pushed
around like a child with assigned papers, reading lists and the
rest. . . . Were they doing this just for money? . . .

Robert, however, was "supportive and cooperative," and
from the day of the plunge, they realized their decision made
sense. If the seminar leaders at the university were dull (they
were regrettably so), Eloise's fellow students were fresh and ar-
gumentative, the ed psych readings often focused on behavior
Eloise recognized and had opinions about, and talking the issues
through with Robert markedly improved dinner table conversation (the children, indulged too long as fixers of talk levels,
learned to listen).

In addition Eloise made an interesting acquaintance and confronted Women's Lib. On its face the link-up looked improbable.
Francine (the acquaintance) and Eloise were of an age, but re-
semblances ended here. Francine lived alone, was bringing up
an eleven-year-old son by herself, worked in the Ed Dean's office,
and took graduate courses in economics and math. She was as-
sertive, with a scoffing, hard-edged note in her voice and a steady
confident expectancy in her glance, as though no matter what
words you spoke to her, you would only confirm an earlier, private understanding she'd arrived at independently. And, most
serious difference, she thought of her life in terms foreign to
Eloise—that is, as a pliant set of circumstances, a stuff that had
no inherent shape, no inevitability, no a priori conditions, forms,
conventions, structures, no *facts* that had to be dealt with on
their (as opposed to your) own terms.

As should be said at once, Eloise at no moment—either in
the relation with Francine, or in her Women's Lib dabblings—saw
herself at the edge of a personal transformation or Breakout. She

pressed for information ("things to read"), felt Francine's force as a person, grasped that Francine's seriousness rested on a hidden foundation—perhaps not the standard substructure of feminism—that could nevertheless be turned into words and considered, and was worth considering. And at no point in the cycle of her tentative involvement with the Lib—whether during her readings in de Beauvoir and Friedan and Lessing (Doris), or as she listened to talk, procedural or therapeutic, at support meetings—at no point was her attitude toward The Cause negative or carping.

But it was touched by skepticism. As this or that sister named real grievances, Eloise was nagged, even amid sympathy, by a notion that the girl might be rating her gifts and deserts too high, or was rebellious in the style of Robert's psychologically troubled, schoolboy Weathermen, or simply lacked the ability to sustain *any* human connection. Eloise's detachment, her tendency to take up a critical-evaluative posture vis-à-vis Francine and the others, sometimes struck her as treacherous. Francine didn't taunt or bait her, none of the girls probed the texture of her life, the Lib cell sessions she attended centered on plans for a free day care center, no silent Quakerish pressure for "conversion" oppressed the room. . . . And yet Eloise did not feel in good faith in their midst.

Oddly, a comparable discomfort bothered her in this period whenever she and Robert talked at length on the subject. For a while it didn't occur to her that duplicity figured in her reporting about Francine or her first few Women's Lib cell meetings. Her way of speaking communicated her responses in their fullness, so she believed. She felt—well, that the meetings were *interesting*. There was extravagance in some of what was said—in the head of steam or hatred occasionally worked up for The Oppressor. There was also considerable self-congratulation and a surprising history of passivity. . . . Why had they put up with what they claimed to have put up with in the past? Eloise wondered aloud to Robert. How could they have been such scared-Aunties, afraid of their own shadows, etc.? At the cell meetings the fiercest speaker about men was a girl who also belonged to one of Eloise's seminars. And in the seminar the girl was cowed,

even meaching—seemingly terrified by a male teacher who neither in mind nor manner was truly intimidating.

But, Eloise would say, at the same time the factual side of
the complaints was impressive. The factual side, she "noted" rea-
sonably to Robert, did seem undeniable and this was, at the very
least (once again)—*interesting*. After a month or two, though, her
casualness and condescension, her willingness to respond to
Robert's questions about whether a lot of dikey types weren't the
ringleaders and so on—all this came to seem to her improper if
not deceitful.

And the twin discomforts—ambiguity before the cell sisters,
and a sense of disloyalty before Robert—at length had an effect:
she and Robert fought one night, no warning signs beforehand
and more ferocity in the air than they'd known before.

It was Robert's "fault"—in the sense that he introduced the
subject which became disputed ground. He was neither facetious
nor dogmatic at first. The children were in, husband and wife
were having coffee in front of the fireplace and Robert com-
menced to explain that he'd been thinking about The Issue (Man
v. Woman) and that he had a theory, he wondered whether the
key wasn't really elementary. His idea, as it turned out, was
creditable—a product of above-average imagination, concern,
earnestness. He'd been reading a magazine piece about a child
rearing experiment at Harvard conducted by Professor Bruner
and others. The part that fascinated him had to do with a typ-
ology of mothers constructed by careful observers—trained psy-
chologists and researchers in pediatrics whose aim was to assess
maternal talents. Robert had been especially struck by a description of a genius mother—skillful, gifted, marvelously apt at teaching infants, developing her children's perceptiveness, increasing
their capacity to interpret experience . . . Robert read a snippet
to Eloise from the description of the woman—an account of her
manner of communicating the concept of (and the word for)
water to a babe-in-arms, as mother and child passed a fountain
in a cab.

And thereafter, perhaps just a shade heavily, Robert elabor-
ated on this theme. The truth was, he said, that to know what
to do in such situations, as the mother knew, required Mind.
From which you could conclude that, properly conceived,

mother's work was no mere affair of diapers and toilet bowls but something embodying intellectual challenge.

—And it's not their fault that they can't see it, Robert added hastily, noticing that Eloise was shaking her head. He naturally assumed that Eloise assumed that he was going to "blame" women—blame Francine, whom he had yet to meet, blame the others in the "interesting" group. Robert assumed this was why Eloise shook her head as he spoke—he held up his hand fore-stalling interruption and tried to make his point clear. He wasn't bringing up the research thing in order to justify some sweet-ness-and-light sermon about creativity and Earth-motherhood. Not at all. He had in mind saying the exact opposite, namely that women's obliviousness to the nature of the job they were doing was inevitable, given their education. Who, Robert asked with a slight and nearly convincing lift of indignation, who taught a mother what her true work consisted of? Where were the in-tellectual and imaginative as contrasted with the sentimental and utilitarian dimensions of the labor made clear? What besides pots and pans did they teach in these stupid home ec courses? What did Dr. Spock offer in the way of nourishment to intellect? All he ever said, as Robert could recall, was: Don't worry, don't fret, don't think, follow your instinct and sleep well. . . . What a travesty! What blasphemy! How could a mother be satisfied with a job thus presented? Everywhere—in novels, ads, on TV, movies —everywhere mothers were shown as ninnies, people who love love love and cope cope cope. Could anybody be blamed for not wanting to live his life on those terms?

Robert had achieved good volume and intensity when he noticed that Eloise was still shaking her head. He was irritated by this observation. He was spurred on to point out—not un-irascibly now, for had he not after all made an effort to perceive, acknowledge and celebrate the dignity of women's work?—he was spurred on to remark about the prevalence of the fantasy that males never did dirty work, never faced unpleasantness or bore-dom on the job. Grading goddam weekly quizzes week after week, year after year, the same asinine mistakes, sly guesses and attempts to deceive . . . Robert hoped Eloise didn't think there was a moment when dealing with other people's vanity and shibboleths and fatuity and irresponsibility didn't bug him and make him want to scream for independence. . . . If she had that crazy idea in her head, if she—

Robert was rising now to a threatening tone ("better get it out of your skull and come into the real world"), but Eloise interrupted. She told him he missed the point. He didn't understand. She told him she was finished with the Lib and hadn't meant to be in it in the first place, never belonged. But her reasons weren't his. She believed these people made a fundamental mistake. They thought women were the most oppressed people and they weren't and women had certain compensations they denied and the cell was nonetheless turning away from real oppression (blacks, poor people) and that to her was the crucial thing—maybe she could understand the rest of it but not that. But as for Robert's "key",—no, it meant he didn't see what they'd been getting at.

Oh yes, oh sure, she acknowledged, his strategy was swell. Brilliant. Dress Mom up, make every mother sort of an assistant pseudo-psychologist, give her a bit of scientific patter about teaching infants, brain facts, eye facts, linguistics. . . . Very clever. Did he actually think that went to the heart of anything? It was Band-aids, mere Band-aids.

They were waking the children now. Robert was furious. He was furious partly at her parody of his proposal, partly because she was out of her known, familiar character. But Eloise wouldn't be shouted down. She repeated that he didn't understand. He was denying women choice—choice was the key. Choice was what they didn't have. It was the culture, it wasn't men. It was history and the way things were, there weren't any villains but there were roles and slots and models and there was terrifically less openness on the girl side, she was conditioned growing up, the world for her was ever so much smaller, less various. . . . And what was Robert's proposal intended to do but just ratify that, make it more palatable? Couldn't he see he wasn't one bit less oppressive—well, not oppressive, she didn't mean to say that. But *continuous* with what existed, no change. It was all the same, more of the same thing. . . . Could he really not see that? . . .

Small potatoes, obviously, as a marital brawl. A modest scrap. "It takes patience to appreciate domestic bliss," Santayana said; "volatile spirits prefer unhappiness." Robert and Eloise didn't prefer unhappiness, worked to restore bliss, and to repeat, in the sequel they did alter their shared life. En route to the improvement, Robert "read up the subject." At the weightier end the materials provided ranged from *The Second Sex* and John Stuart Mill ("On the Subjection of Women") and Kate Millett to Gunnar Myrdal's *An American Dilemma* (that book proved to have an Appendix drawing the parallel between beliefs about black people and beliefs about women), and from Engels' *Origins of the Family, Private Property and the State* (suggestive account of the emergence of status differentiation among men and women and of the development of women as a form of property), to a twenty-year-old essay by the sociologist Everett Hughes on "The Marginal Man" which included among other observations, this:

> The traditional roles of neither women nor Negro include that of physician. Hence when either of them becomes a physician the question arises whether to treat her or him as a physician or as woman or as Negro. . . . On their part, there is the problem whether, in a given troublesome situation, to act completely as physician or in the other role. This is their dilemma.

On the less tasking side the material included issues of Protestant denominational magazines, issues of *Life, Look,* the *Sunday Times Magazine,* the *Village Voice, Ramparts* and a dozen other popular publications, a file of Women's Lib newsletters from Boston and New York cells and subgroups, an article in the London *Sunday Times* called "The Third World War: Women Against Men," a mimeographed 40-page single-spaced essay called "Toward a Female Liberation Movement," in which two southerners argue that women must leave existing radical organizations and fight their own battles first.

There was amusement—occasionally guilty—in this reading project. Robert grinned at the determination of Women's Lib writers to eschew euphemisms and gentility when discussing sexual matters. (Making love was invariably called "screwing" in official movement prose.) The heavily stressed Black Power/ Woman Power analogy led to funny borrowings and coinages. (Accommodaters and temporizers within the Women's Lib movement were spoken of as Aunt Thomasinas.) The names of fringe

groups or cells within the movement were often piquant. (A
Boston cell is called Bread and Roses: "women operatives" picket-
ing a Massachusetts shoe factory in the late nineteenth century
bore signs that read, "Give us Bread and Roses." And there was
the famous New York liberationist society called SCUM—Society
for Cutting Up Men, and the Women's International Terrorist
Conspiracy from Hell, called WITCH.) The scope of the effort
to break old habits and assumptions in sexual matters also made
Robert smile. ("We have got to stop throwing around terms like
'fag,' 'pimp,' 'queer' and 'dike' to reassure men of our absolute
loyalty to them," wrote a Judith Brown in one 1968 paper on
Female Liberation. "This is the language which helps to insure
that each man has his female slave and that each woman event-
ually becomes one.") And while Robert felt the humiliating force
of remarks addressed to would-be women radicals in student and
black militant organizations, he was too "conditioned" to keep a
completely straight face. (In 1964 Stokely Carmichael held publicly that "the only position for women in SNCC is prone." In
the Columbia student rebellion of 1968 a male leader in occupied
Fayerweather Hall demanded that the girls in the place volun-
teer for cooking duty.)

And there was also much that caused him depression—the
rigor of the resistance, for example, to so-called enslaving senti-
mentalities about motherhood. Was it not pointlessly, pathetically
reductive always to speak of having babies as "dropping children"? ("I think we can defer dropping children on cultural
command. . . .") Was it not needlessly fierce to equate affection
between the sexes with pure fantasy? The London *Times* essay,
pro-WLM, reported that:

> "We're tired of talking about sex," said [Boston] WLM leader
> Roxanne Dunbar; "the subject of orgasm doesn't come up at our
> meetings. Sex is just a commodity, a programmed activity, it is
> not a basic need." At least until after the revolution, the . . .
> group advises women to look to their comrades for an affection
> which does not depend upon fantasy and false eyelashes. "And
> if, despite all this, genital tensions persist," they advise in an
> article called "On Celibacy," "you can still masturbate."

Robert never did adjust, furthermore, to the vision of the
male workday as a continuum of excitement. Over and over

again, echoing the thesis of *The Second Sex,* Women's Lib writers declared that "a woman's role as a wife and [as] the socializer of children acts as a stunting influence upon her creativity," whereas a man's role in the job world liberates his powers:

> . . . men are encouraged [wrote Laurel Limpus in *This Magazine Is About Schools*] to play out their lives in the realm of transcendence, whereas women are confined to immanence. This simply means that men work, create, do things, are in positions of authority, create their own histories; whereas women are confined to the home, where their function is not to create, but to maintain: Women keep house and raise children.

And he was equally hostile to the WLM practice of tracing every form of social and cultural malaise to the single source—"Enslavement of women."

But if his reading persuaded him that WLM rhetoric and propaganda was often as shrill and naïve as that of SDS pamphlets and papers, it also showed him the inadequacy of his own previous understanding of the issues. And it was Eloise's point about choice—amplified, reiterated, intensified in the literature of the movement—that ultimately defined his mistakes. It mattered, to be sure, that wage scales were hopelessly unfair (women earn 60 cents for every dollar paid to men in comparable jobs). It mattered that the causes regarded as central by NOW (the National Organization for Women)—among them, expansion of child care centers and abortion repeal—were, in his view, just causes. It mattered that the swiftest glance at any list of Women's Lib projects in a newsletter—a course in elementary car repair, a project to circulate information about good and bad gynecologists, a course in Women and Their Bodies, classes in Karate, formation of a church group to help with "problem pregnancies"— quickened awareness of the variety of modes of "arranged" womanly defenselessness.

And it mattered too that everywhere in Women's Lib writing you came on bits of unacknowledged evidence about how it went "back then," early in the marriage, for the Young Mother— while the complacent Young Father winked away the truth:

> What hits a new mother the hardest is not so much the increased work load as the lack of sleep. . . . If you have never been awakened and required to function at one in the morning and

again at three, then maybe at seven, or some such schedule, you can't imagine the agony of it. All of a woman's muscles ache and they respond with further pain when touched. She is generally cold and unable to get warm. Her reflexes are off. She startles easily, ducks moving shadows, and bumps into stationary objects. Her reading rate takes a precipitous drop. She stutters and stammers, groping for words to express her thoughts, sounding barely coherent—somewhat drunk. . . . In response to all the aforementioned symptoms she is always close to tears. . . .

This lack of sleep is rarely mentioned in the literature relating to the Tired Mother Syndrome. Doctors recommend to women with newborn children that they attempt to partially compensate for this loss of sleep by napping during the day. With one child that may be possible, with several small ones it's sort of a sick joke. This period of months or years of forced wakefulness and "maternal" responsibility seems to have a long-range if not permanent effect on a woman's sleeping habits. She is so used to listening for the children she is awakened by dogs, cats, garbage men, neighbors' alarm clocks, her husband's snoring. Long after her last child gives up night feedings she is still waking to check on him. She is worried about his suffocating, choking, falling out of bed, etc. . . . Enforced wakefulness is the handmaiden and necessary precursor to serious brainwashing. . . . A mother is embarrassed by her halting speech, painfully aware of her lessened ability to cope with things, of her diminished intellectual prowess. She relies more heavily than ever on her husband's support, helping hand, love. And he in turn gently guides her into the further recesses of second class citizenship.

But above all it was the idea of Conditioning, the creation by glances, gestures, nuances of talk beyond counting of the classic "female pathology," that moved Robert on from his simplicities. The Lib Movement was rich in documentation of the conditioning processes. Writer after writer rummaged in her past, hunted out childhood details with a bearing on the making of modern femininity. "I grew up," wrote Vivian Gornick in *The Village Voice*.

I grew up in the certainty that if my brother went to college, I too could go to college; and, indeed, he did, and I in my turn did too. We both read voraciously from early childhood on, and we were both encouraged to do so. We both had precocious and outspoken opinions and neither of us was ever discouraged from uttering them. We both were exposed early to unionist radicalism and neither of us met with opposition when, separately, we experimented with youthful political organizations. And yet somewhere along the line my brother and I managed to receive an utterly different education regarding ourselves and our own expectations from life. He was taught many things but what he learned was the need to develop a kind of inner necessity. I was taught many things but what I learned, ultimately, was that it was the prime vocation of my life to prepare myself for the love of a good man. . . .

How did I learn this? How? I have pondered this question 1000 times. Was it really that explicit? Was it laid out in lessons strategically planned and carefully executed? Was it spooned down my throat at regular intervals? No. It wasn't. I have come finally to understand that the lessons were implicit and they took place in 100 different ways, in a continuous day-to-day exposure to an *attitude,* shared by all, about women, about what kind of creatures they were and what kind of lives they were meant to live; the lessons were administered not only by my parents but by the men and women, the boys and girls, all around me who, of course, had been made in the image of this attitude.

And Mrs. Gornick and numberless others rendered this conditioning with remarkable fullness for Robert—and, to his credit, he saw. He grasped the meaning of a blinkered youth, understood that the first "inequality" was in the range of openness to possibility, and that, in his own world of unconscious assumptions, domesticity was still somehow felt not as an option among options for women, but as a dictate of nature, a form or law preceding individual variation and retaining its force no matter how often or successfully "transgressed."

As for the sequel: no major behavioral changes. (This tale cannot gladden revolutionaries.) The marriage of Robert and Eloise was not radicalized. Robert didn't contribute funds to the woman's commune building campaign, he didn't divide the housework with Eloise, didn't sign for hours in the child care center. The habit of interdependency and of humor and of habit itself laid its strong hand on Robert's Illumination—accommodated it to old harmonies, fitted it to past affection and need. What happened was simply that husband and wife came at moments to hold the idea of marriage in their mind differently, changed their relation to an area of life once frozen in cultural (unexamined) form. Robert and Eloise catch themselves often, of course, returning to staleness and routine. They assent without thinking to some commonplace assertion of "prejudice" against woman or of Shock at youth's contempt for marriage. . . . They slide off into standard-form, ready-made understandings.

But they also on other occasions interrupt themselves, they touch a fresh intuition of marriage as a creation, a human invention; they perceive woman's "natural" domesticity as in truth a decision, an act deserving a decent rung in the hierarchy of conscious choice. In a word: Robert and Eloise now inhabit, from time to time, a world in which the separateness of women's work and men's isn't divinely ordained, any more than femininity (softness, lovingness) and masculinity (hard, cold) are Given, like The Law. They have ventilated their experience, acknowledged arbitrariness: they've looked out on the face of possibility and neither blanched nor run.

From which what follows? Trust Women's Lib, impossible for it to do harm? Trust the steady even good sense of loving mates, it cannot be overmatched?

Too cheery. The abstract, damnation-dealing fury of some Women's Lib cells does indeed resemble that of Weathermen gatherings. And, as may as well be acknowledged, a dozen irrelevant frustrations pump energy to that fury. This woman married a dull man, this one a mean man, this one a loafer, this woman grew up timid and found her tongue only at thirty-five, this woman lacked touch with children, this woman mistakes her Phi Beta Kappa key for permanent intellectual distinction, this woman's a compulsive scrubber, this woman had too few desires and too little humor and too much lust for make-work to relish the rich freedoms of subsidized life. . . . This woman shuddered all her days before people who (if she but would have spoken) would have delighted in her very voice. . . . Within women thus afflicted, the new revolutionary rhetoric nourishes resentments and self-deceptions that are worse than ludicrous or pitiable, for they damage children's lives as well as parents'.

But it's one thing to ante up these concessions, and another to join the male chorus of mockers that's lately begun to swell. The case is that the Lib idea has great honing powers—and whether or not marriage is, as the wise man said, the only adventure open to the cowardly, it plainly ought to have an edge.

And an edge sharpens when unconscious assumption is confronted, and when the risks and promise of choice and freedom come clear. Say it straight: there's a loony fringe here as elsewhere on the Mod Scene—and there's also a notion that can be well-used: not a weapon, not a nostrum, but a means of opening ourselves, locating the "competing models," sounding the depth of our still insufficiently acknowledged personal responsibility for the terms of our daily life.

Seeing with a Husband's Eye

Hear out another contemporary domestic story: heavier in masculine fact. Janet S. is a mother in her late thirties—two junior high children and one pre-schooler. Her best friend and former neighbor Carol is in her mid-twenties, with a toddler and an infant. The friendship between the two grew up in the usual ways —morning coffee, sitting exchanges, gardening information exchanges, book-borrowing, egg-borrowing, child-rearing talk, occasional joint family picnics. . . . But it had a special character, deriving mainly from the two mothers' shared (and amused) satisfaction in their own "domesticity." Neither mother was champing to claim her independence, or impatient to complete a graduate degree, or frustrated by an interrupted career; each was intelligent, moderately ironical, more or less content. Janet and Carol joked sometimes about each other's lack of militancy and bitterness, but they were loyal to it, pleased by each other's easy enjoyment and relish of the terms of her life.

And then a blow fell—a serious and hurtful blow. Carol's

husband inherited a house ten miles closer to the city, the couple moved, and within weeks Carol's husband left her. (He took an apartment by himself in the same town, returned at night to put the children to bed, but acted to Carol, as she said, as though "I wasn't even here.") Janet, for her part, was bewildered and depressed. She knew and liked Carol's husband—how could he suddenly turn and become somebody else, a wholly different person? She talked at length but inconclusively (and unhelpfully, she gloomily believed) with Carol. She tried to offer comfort—but what good were words? When she spoke to Philip, her own husband, he agreed it was terrible, awful—a terrible thing. —Then he pointed out there was nothing anyone could do.

Janet didn't accept this. She grew angry at her own helplessness. A week after hearing the news she asked Carol whether she had thought of suggesting to her estranged husband that they go away somewhere together—take a trip, try to see what their real problems were, talk it out. . . . Janet admitted it sounded stilted, artificial—marriage counselorish. But still it might help. How could you be sure? Carol and her husband had never had a chance to be together, they'd been too involved, worrying about children, money, household problems . . . She, Janet, could easily take the children. It'd be fun for her little girl. . . . At least Carol ought to ask and find out whether he'd think about it, why not do that? Didn't it make sense?

Do such schemes ever make sense? Perhaps—but for present purposes what counts isn't the merits of the idea. It is rather that the moment Janet advanced it—or spoke about having advanced it—a gap yawned between her and her husband. Janet explained that it had just come over her, she had to do something, it was crazy for these children to break up, not even telling each other why. . . . It didn't make sense. But Philip (the husband) was stony. He nodded as she spoke, he said again how hard it was to know what was right. He sighed, shook his head. Janet knew he was, in her phrase, "clearing out"—cutting off from her momentarily. They weren't connecting. Philip wasn't beginning to say what was in his mind. He would have liked to have been able to utter his thoughts. It would have been good for them both, good for Janet—if he could have made her understand. And because knowing even a sliver of what goes on when this "cutting-

out" experience occurs even briefly, and because the movement
of masculine feeling too seldom comes into full sight, it's perhaps
forgivable (forgetting Janet and Carol and Carol's problem abruptly) to try to violate Philip's silence at this instant—to come
closer to him, to try to spell out at least a little of his inward
response.

That response is complex, naturally. The first thing Philip
would have said, if he'd been able to speak his mind, wouldn't
have had a negative ring. He would have said that Janet's idea
seemed to him a perfect embodiment of her character, of what
she was as a person. For while he too was responsive to suffering, while he too "hated to see people hurt," it was stronger in
her than in him to believe that "something could be done," and
that it was any one single individual's responsibility to see that
it was done. He often had this comparative sense of Janet's
"moral superiority." That's to say, he often imagined her as "vir-
tuous enough for the two of them," as the conscience of the
household, as an inviolable repository of unselfishness and gen-
erosity. He felt genuine humility, even an awe. Here was a human being, his mate, who would put herself out endlessly, un-
hesitatingly, uncomplainingly, for her friend.

Yet there was a negative side and it had nothing to do with
"minding your own business." It had everything to do with the
difference in their situations—his and Janet's. There was a hint
of envy in his head, he admitted that—a rueful notion that if certain features of her life (those that made it possible for her seriously to care what happened to Carol in the first place) were
part of his, the job of breadwinning would be easier. There was
also a degree of pity. He pitied her not because she'd be taking
on a heavier burden of menial work, caring for someone else's
children—it was just for a few days. No, he pitied her for reasons
having much to do with the difference in range and interest between her life-satisfactions and his own.

So little of his, so much of her pleasure, depended upon acts
of kindness, self-forgetfulness. Think of everything she had to
remember! Her head had been stored over all their child-rearing
years with incredible material—the precise location of a Skipper
doll in the laundry room, the outdoor as opposed to indoor
basketball, an eleven-year-old's left boot, dentist appointment,

French teacher's last name . . . Astonishment at her memory, the
feeling that every individual item of its content stood as irre-
futable proof of her concern for the needs and happiness of
others—that was one root of Philip's feeling for her moral distinction.

But it was also—coming back again to the evaded, the ambiguous, the negative element in his thoughts and feelings—it was
also a root of his condescension. Philip saw Janet as someone
who believed that when tragedy struck, you could do something
about it. She believed, in other words, in order, and in her own
potency as a human being. —And why not? he would ask himself with a kind of wry tenderness. Why shouldn't Janet? What
else does she know? Fixed in a cozy, established, unvarying relationship to herself and others—children, neighbors, habitual
round of callers (postman, milkman, dry cleaner)—she was someone who knew who, what and where she was, at any given
moment. Her "identity" was ceaselessly confirmed and recon-
firmed throughout the day. Her responsibilities, her appropriate
style of behavior, weren't in flux. Her survival didn't depend on
her capacity to remake herself for unprecedented situations, unpredictable crises. The terms of her job allowed for unity and
coherence and comprehension. When accident or misfortune—
some eruption of chaos—appeared in her world, it had a known
face and a name: it was somebody. It was a failure that, no matter how infuriating or depressing, wasn't felt (by her) as mys-
terious or blank or beyond human clarification or confrontation.
Enormously kind, sweet, she was also, in a deep sense, an innocent: she *had no conception of the quantity of impersonality,
of sheer mechanical uncaringness and discontinuity abroad in the
general world.*

—Oh, what he wouldn't give (he thought on bad days) for a
portion of that innocence! And oh what he'd give to break out
of his own impotence. Traveling, for example—think about that a
while! Breakdowns, unexplained delays, sudden layovers in
Kansas City, extended waits for "a piece of hydraulic equipment
being flown in from Elmira," enforced desultory weary conversation with equally powerless strangers in boarding areas . . .
If you had that experience, you knew how easy it was to have
personal identity and significance emptied out, how ridiculous it

was to pretend that when things collapsed, the sane response was to seek the causes, assign responsibility, right the balance, take steps, correct the situation, etc. No, Philip wasn't equating the breakdown of a marriage with delays on a landing strip. No, he wasn't out for a bath of self-pity. He just meant that, while a traveler might be able to think of himself as effective and potent in some (non-travel) situations, he was also damned well acquainted with a world in which he was useless, incapable of raising his hand to any purpose.

And that was one thing he *knew* Janet didn't know. Again and again in her talk—not alone about friends or about local disasters, either—he heard in Janet's very tone that, rich as her sympathy was, she hadn't a direct intuition of what true powerlessness actually felt like, how it made you turn up your hands at life itself. . . .

Nor was the thing he was thinking about just an on-the-road problem. This fundamental lack of order-continuity-steadiness of self was the rule everywhere. Philip's working world was, he believed, one in which survival demanded ceaseless remaking of behavior and appearance and tone. Continually—yet always abruptly, without warning—you were adapting to facts of power and place. One moment diffidence, the next authority and control, no gradual transitions between. Janet found it shocking that Carol's Roger could "be so different overnight," could become something she never knew him to be. How much did she know about *his*, Philip's, variations of personality? See him in his own office, door closed, dealing with a subordinate, chiding the man, urging him on to a better performance, using any style of intimidation that looked promising—and amidst this effort the phone rings—his own boss speaking, cracking in his ear, and the problem is to manage a posture of deference with dignity that doesn't undercut authority with the junior across the desk from him.

These standard strains weren't part of Janet's life. (How *could* Roger [Carol's husband] do it? she asked. It's just not *like* him, etc.) She could believe in the consistency of human selves, their relative openness with each other. Direct dealing was, in her mind, the norm of life, not the exception. And while the very foundation of this faith was a personal quality of idealism, there was no denying that the quality was, face it, "innocent."

And the same had to be said, didn't it? about her implicit notion that change on this order—the breakup of her friend's whole existence—was somehow unthinkable. Philip knew that Janet "knew" abstractly that the age they lived in was becoming increasingly disorderly. But *how* exactly did she know this? How did her knowledge feel from the inside? He wasn't exactly sure what he meant here, couldn't get it wholly clear. It had to do vaguely with the degree in which a vivid apprehension of "possibility" was a constant of his daily life—in a way it couldn't be a constant of hers. True, there were openings in Janet's day: by agility and flexibility and "careful managing," much that wasn't merely domestic could be "fitted in." But she did have to be on call as a mother, she was obliged either to care for the children herself or to provide an alternative sitter whose services were of short duration, and—most important—she had to see her job and its responsibilities in more or less the same terms as long as he and she continued as man and wife. Being his wife and the mother of his children meant a prescribed routine of cooking, cleaning, shopping, housekeeping interruptible only by effortfully-arranged-for holidays. And therefore she didn't live at close quarters with the realization that, at no notice, "everything might be otherwise than it is"—or that implicit in any particular way of having one's life experience was the possibility of having that experience in multiple other ways.

Whereas precisely this realization governed Philip's understanding of "how things went." Granted the sense of possibility for a husband often amounted only to a close look at lives different from his own. A tax lawyer momentarily peeks inside the lifestyle and personality of a film star. An economics teacher is taken into a circle of top White House advisors. A small-town businessman serves with students and professors on a board of trustees of a community college. A minister is appointed to a governor's committee on prison reform. An ad man finds himself merchandising a political candidate . . . But experience of this sort provides a different window on the world, access as a spectator to unfamiliar ways of thinking, feeling, valuing, and therefore it can work, as Philip knew, as a prod to active invention of alternative schemes of life.

And, given an urban setting—hotel availability, for example, drinking lunches, commuter disasters—such prods continually stimulate an idea of fidelity as a choice, a decision taken among a variety of competing options. Philip worked with a man he knew to be living what was called "a double life." He knew another man well—an executive for a soft drink company—who, on a series of business trips to a Caribbean island, arranged an entirely new life for himself and his secretary, developing and testing out an alternative existence in a new marriage with the "other woman," before announcing to his wife that he wanted a divorce. Hateful and deceitful as they are, think of the intricacies of such an arrangement! What "housewife" could have conceived it?

What's more, Philip thought, it's not unlikely that in one way or another Carol's husband had behaved as he had done because of the prompting of *his* sense of possibility. Perhaps the man's very "restlessness" arose from his feeling for the remoteness of his life conditions from hers—from her "innocence," her conception of life-transformation as The Unthinkable. Philip felt he couldn't say this, of course—not without, as he told himself, wounding or frightening Janet. He couldn't begin to speak of the paradoxical elements of the situation. He was inhibited about acknowledging that the neutral, mechanized, impersonal and discontinuous world of work roused in *everybody* an appetite for meaningful connection—an appetite that sometimes led not to heightened appreciation of family, home and hearth, but gave birth to "alliances of desperation" . . . love affairs ventured as a defense against the harshness of the daytime business world. And whenever he felt this inhibition—against showing forth to his wife the truths hidden from her by her "inexperience"—he suffered a qualm of secret guilt. But it did not cause him to speak. The strong restraint compelling him not quite to credit her goodness at full adult value also enforced him to keep silent on the matter their parents in their day spoke of as Temptation. And that restraint was in part a sense of her as a child.*

---

* This way of seeing—odd, fond, parental tenderness—has a past in countless bad movies and many good poems, novels, plays. (The paternal voice sounds clearly in Adam's voice in John Milton's *Paradise Lost*, as he warns Eve against leaving his side even briefly as they work in the Garden. And there's Dickens—and Ibsen—and Hemingway, who delighted in calling grown women "Daughter.") And, as anybody would guess, the feeling isn't

Is it feasible to argue with the Philips of the world, show them that their versions of their wives' psyches are travesties of the facts? Is it useful to remind them that Janet's world is by no means as manageable—or as human in scale—as it's commonly taken to be? For a mother with clear values, steady concern for the holistic development of her children, and a feeling for central decencies and values, the places away from home into which her children go forth are indeed filled with unreckonable, unopposable force—and with a specter of Possibility far from benign. Her children's education occurs, much of it, in settings that can seldom be monitored—not in classrooms but with friends or in front of TV or with shaky or neurotic elders. Some of the latter may on their face be harmless, easily warned against. All, however, are capable of instilling against a mother's will, without her knowledge, a conviction that success or victory justifies any course of action, or that accumulating possessions and tending one's own vanity are the highest forms of human preoccupation, or that this or that variety of rebellious, unconventional, non-conformist and dangerous self-expression is "smart." Philip's Janet knows, not less well than he, that her hopeful idea of herself as a potent, responsible, competent and effectively caring elder can at any moment be proved to be a fantasy; she knows the erupting force of possibility on her own terms—and these aren't much more comforting than his.

Why then can't he be told this and saved from his errors? Why can't a husband be reasoned with about the excessively myth-ridden conception of wifedom presently ruling his mind? Why can't he be taught that bad sequels like that faced by Carol and Roger might be avoided if husbands helped wives to prevent themselves from being thought of as happy peaceful custodians of a "simpler world," islands (whereon all forms of good

---

as simple as it looks. It isn't, for instance, a mere matter of dependency. A wife's motive in entering the job market may be to make her spouse accept her as an adult sharing full economic responsibility. Yet he is as likely as not to misread her motive, and see her as someone victimized like a child by romantic fantasies about the excitement of a workaday office world. Discovering how "a sense of her as a child" now operates in a husband's mind, glimpsing the attitudes, assumptions and misperceptions that nourish and strengthen it, can't be done without peering intently at "the specific situation."

and bad take shape as personal deeds), oases, changeless utopias, doll's houses, playrooms?

Best again to speak bluntly: the reason it's hard to teach is that when a husband doesn't have a sense of his wife as a child, he often has a sense of her as himself. At home, a little after being shocked by the news about Carol, and irked by Janet's response, Philip doesn't hold fast to his critical detachment from her: he does not continue to see her as a child. A moment like the one spoken of here induces in him a temporary feeling of separateness—like the separateness that comes over him on the road, or even in the office in a moment of crisis or insecurity. But the spirit of detachment doesn't survive long in his living room.

When they are together, in fact, it would be most true to say that Philip doesn't actually see Janet, doesn't think about her as separate from him. How can he do that, how can he *think* about her, see her as a subject, an occasion for analysis, speculation, consecutive reasoning? She isn't outside him then. Only under exceptional circumstances—as at the instant she's telling him of a breakup—can he undertake to objectify her. Minutes later she is what she invariably is, when they are together—a part of his store of experienced, potentially recollectable actuality, an assumption or condition, not Somebody Over There Across The Room. Her responses, thoughts, kindnesses, are part of his mind. He knows them, feels proprietorial about them before she speaks; her positions even in their private arguments constitute dissent he organized and underwrote (in the interest of a healthy society). His powerful habitual attachment to her, his committed loyalty, his inward understanding (at home) that nothing—nothing on earth—will alter the terms of their relation to each other, denies her the kind of freedom and self-sufficiency possessed by most other people he knows.

And, while he is with her, this same powerful attachment somehow denies freedom to him as well. The fact of their union —a clear glass bell set down over them—enormously outweighs any "merely personal" gesture or thought or opinon or illumination flowing from within either of them. It muffles subjectivity, renders speech unimportant if not needless, drains significance from thought about each other. Who needs such thought? What is the point of it? We're *married.*

If a formula is wanted, it might go thus: a husband's "thoughts" about his wife *may* take the form of a "sense of her as a child," and, when they do, this way of thinking can be, simultaneously, a maze, an altar, a prison, and a will of the wisp. But those thoughts themselves are forever receding under the pressure of the longing to luxuriate in taking self *and* other for granted, feeling coextensive with her, recovering from the "short disease, myself," becoming "a couple." And therefore to probe into "what a husband thinks,"—in or out of the Lib cell or support group—is to come close to the edge of a problem that isn't finally a matter of masculine condescension, repression, or infidelity, and that isn't truly domestic or social in nature. It is, instead, the problem of our inner call for a release from separateness and mentalism, for a world of profound not casual linkage: the deep, human, ever-increasingly-difficult-to-satisfy need for a mode of retreat from self-love.

Ecological Summons:
Change Your Life

—And then came "ecology:" newest prod to possibility, latest incitement to self-transformation, strongest mocker of men's past. A fresh item, a hot media ticket, the "ecology story" has been battered by journalistic cliché almost from the beginning. One paper plays the handy Political Angles, separating ground floor people (Senator Muskie) from me-tooers (President Nixon), noting that the cause made "strange bedfellows," etc. (Girl Scouts, Weathermen and Birchers singing the self-same antipollution blues). Another digs the Personalities—"dedicated, hornrimmed" Barry Commoner, "outdoorsy, glamour-puss" David Brower . . . And everywhere pseudo-events are laid on for electronic newsmen (car burials, Earth Days, bottle pickups and the like)—items occasioning "major speeches," "photographic essays," "public affairs specials" that rock the issue to the beat of Now.

Yet despite the energies expended on conventionalizing and trivializing the discovery of the abuse of nature, the thing hasn't gone under. It was quick to work its way through the bread-and-circus scene of fast-breaking news, information, The Latest to the status of a continuing, regularly updated story. And the evidence at hand testifies that ecological crisis may soon rank as the most crucial of all influences on the deep structure of men's self-discontent.

As goes without saying, the influence of the discovery in question could stop well short of that impact and still be no negligible force. In the world of teaching and learning, for instance, the focus on survival has underlined both the urgency and mutual interdependence of pedagogical themes separately teased and deprecated by the knowing in the recent past. Professor Commoner argues that "You can't look at turbidity in a stream intelligently without having some knowledge about the banks of the stream and the forest that's growing twenty-five yards away." And, as *The New York Times* environmental correspondent observed, after surveying developments in university ecology action centers, awareness of this truth is encouraging the replacement of "the closed-shop compartmentalization of the traditional 'disciplines'—such as biology, chemistry, physics, botany, and geology—[with] an eclectic approach." Support for interdisciplinary work has in turn nourished the cause of "experiential education"—studies that move out from classroom and library situations into the field, confronting the social and political (as well as natural) intricacies of immediate experience. And the result has been the reanimation of an educational ideal to which nobody but the lowly commencement speaker has given lip service for decades: The Whole Man, the scholar-citizen determined not only to know but to connect his knowledge with the moral imperatives of community concern. Doubtless the dignity and interconnectedness of these themes should always have been ungrudgingly granted. But it wasn't, and the rehabilitation of the themes stands high among the significant, visible, public consequences of the environmental revolution thus far.

But the visible public effects of that revolution outside the academy are, of course, far more momentous. The most obvious of these has been the intensification, throughout the general culture, of belief in the uniqueness of the age—its discontinuity with yesterday, its character as a period without precedent. The rhetoric of Apocalypse and moral melodrama has, true enough, played a part in persuading men of this uniqueness. The national coordinator of Environmental Action declares that:

> America is the new Robber Baron. . . . America has become indifferent to life. . . . If 50,000 people are killed, if ten million starve, if an entire country is laid waste—we have learned to tuck the information into the proper file and write the affair off as a mistake.

The editors of *The Progressive* declare in a special issue that "a new Four Horsemen . . . are riding relentlessly on their mission of destruction." The *Saturday Review* warns that:

> Lake Erie is dead. The beaches at Santa Barbara are deserted. The air in New York is dangerous to breathe. We are drowning in a sea of swill; in a normal year the United States produces 142 million tons of smoke and fumes, seven million junked cars, twenty million tons of waste paper, forty-eight billion used cans, and fifty trillion gallons of industrial sewage . . . a population that is still increasing like an uncontrollable cancer on the surface of the globe.

Paul Ehrlich, the Stanford biologist, presents horrific scenarios for the future:

> SCENARIO III.   In 1974 the United States government finally realizes that the food-population balance in much of Asia, Africa, and South America is such that most areas cannot attain self-sufficiency. American expeditionary forces are withdrawn from Vietnam and Thailand, and the United States announces it will no longer send food to India, Egypt, and some other countries which it considers beyond hope. A moderate food rationing program is instituted in the United States. It further announces that food production will be increased only so long as the increase can be accomplished without damage to the environment of the North American continent. . . . Famine and food riots sweep Asia. In China, India, and other areas of Asia, central governments weaken and then disappear. . . . Most of the countries of Africa and South America slide backward into famine and local warfare. . . . In the United Nations, the United States, Canada, Russia, Japan, Australia, and the Common Market countries set up a machinery for "area rehabilitation" which will involve simultaneous population control, agricultural development, and limited industrialization, to be carried out jointly in select sections in Asia, Africa, and South America. The plan is to be initiated in 1985, when it is calculated that the major die-back will be over, using famine relief stations as bases for both facilities and personnel. . . .

If the voices addressing ecological crises spoke only in such tones, the present sense of living in an "incomparable" historical moment, would be less widely diffused than it is: tonal extremism, in the defense of truth, is a great incitement to skepticism. But many spokesmen for the ecological cause say their piece moderately, coolly, with no intent to inflame—yet nevertheless press just as firmly the point that mankind cannot have known an equivalent crisis before. Professor Commoner speaks restrainedly in *Science and Survival* (1966): "As a biologist, I have reached this conclusion: we have come to a turning point in the human habitation of the earth." The UN Secretary-General, U Thant, matches Commoner's sobriety with his own: "For the first time in the history of mankind, there is arising a crisis of worldwide proportions involving developed and developing countries alike—the crisis of human environment. . . . It is becoming apparent that if current trends continue, the future of life on earth could be endangered." Professor Kenneth Boulding, the economist, remarks—in the course of an effort at characterizing differences between "then" and now—that "neither the American, nor the French, nor the Russian revolutions created fundamental changes in the state of man [as the present situation has done], and the ideologies which supported [those revolutions] are quite inadequate to bear the weight of this enormous transition which we face. . . ." In short, certainty that the age stares straight into an Absolute Unknown echoes and reechoes throughout the new ecological literature, and can't be dismissed as self-hyping hysteria.

If there were nothing more in the equation than this certainty, tracking the cultural impact of the environmental cause back to substantive realities in individual human feeling would be less difficult and less troubling. The point of rest would be—once again—the famous generation gap: the prime change effected in the feeling-life of men might seem a simple matter of new strains on sympathy and confidence between youth and age. "Awareness of ecological crisis as a wholly new fact of life—a fact of which older generations could not conceivably have a sound grasp—confirmed the thesis of Dr. Margaret Mead that a reversal of generational roles, establishing the young as teachers and the aged as pupils, was the characteristic mark of the times." A formula of that sort could serve well enough to bring primary cultural dimensions into view.

But, as it happens, that formula is inadequate. For the most telling human and psychological consequences of the environmental revolution lie not in restructured generational relationships, but, instead, in the extraordinary demands that this revolution lays upon men of every age to achieve detachment from self and culture. The demands in question aren't usually formulated, to be sure, in these terms. Confronted with the task of explaining what is necessary for survival, the leaders of the cause seldom speak first of detachment. Professor Commoner calls for a new means of salvation: "This, I believe, is the urgency of the environmental crisis—we must determine, now, to develop, in the next decade, the new means of our salvation." The *Times'* Gladwin Hill speaks of the need for a rebellion—"a sudden, remarkable, spontaneous rebellion not of one group against another so much as of everybody against the physical conditions to which two centuries of promiscuous 'progress' have brought us. . . ." Senator Gaylord Nelson calls for a "new citizenship," and the head of the Rockefeller Foundation, Dr. George Harrar, plumps for a "new environmental ethic."

But implicit in every address to the problem (and explicit in most) is the requirement that men raise to the level of consciousness myths, values, profound unexamined assumptions governing Western attitudes toward life—in a word, that they teach themselves to objectify their culture. "There appears to be only one viable approach," according to the editors of the *Population Bulletin:*

> This is the long uphill route of encouraging the American people to modify their basic attitudes and behavior so that instead of idealizing large families in the abstract and creating them in flesh and blood, we will prefer small ones and act upon our preferences; so that instead of promoting forms of economic growth which will increasingly pollute our living space, we will insist that we clean up as we go, no matter what the cost; so that instead of measuring our welfare by the amount of our consumption, we will become deeply concerned about enhancing the quality and preserving the variety of life in the momentum of our society.

Can the task of "modifying basic attitudes" begin until "basic attitudes" are laid out to plain view? Is there any way of carrying this work through without disentangling the "attitudes" from their tight relationships with every sector of the belief system, excising layers of inexpressible myth and symbol, objectifying them, hypostatizing them? It's common, as might be expected, for leaders advocating exactly this step to speak as though the job were more or less routine—no need for anxiety or bitter wounds of self. "At this critical juncture," says Dr. Harrar equably, "it would be well for man to question the validity of his attitudes toward nature and to consider seriously the desirability and wisdom of formulating a new ethic for dealing with his natural environment which would transcend most of the values we have traditionally held concerning the world." And the note of agonizing reappraisal is equally absent from Senator Nelson's voice:

> Restoring our environment and establishing quality on a par with quantity as a goal of American life would require a reshaping of our values, sweeping changes in the performance and goals of our institutions . . . a humanizing and redirection of our technology. . . . There is a great need and growing support for the introduction of new values in our society. . . .

But here and there among the ecological spokesmen, a few writers are awed by the very conception of a "transformation of values." (Professor Boulding speaks of the "enormous intellectual and moral task which lies ahead of mankind.")

And even if such voices didn't exist, the scope and nature of the work wouldn't be hidden from us. For the case is, as all readers of literature and students of history know, that the public men now charging us to remake culture and personhood are far from speaking a new tongue. The voice of anger against the dehumanization of the Earth has resounded in letters and philosophy for longer than two centuries. The great protest on behalf of the organic view of nature that Professor Whitehead heard in the romantic poets has been a ground theme of literature from the "romantic movement" to the present. The will to criticize the industrial civilization, to view its gifts as ambiguous, to oppose the despoliation of the landscape, is a norm everywhere in American literature from Hawthorne to Fitzgerald and after (see the invaluable work of Professor Leo Marx in this area). "Civilization" has been understood as in process of destroying itself by virtually every major English writer from Blake to Lawrence, and the need for "a new ethic" has been urged by scores of writers contributing, over the past century, to the debate about culture and society in that country. (William Morris was already anticipating, a century ago, "the day [when] there is a serious strike of workmen against the poisoning of the air with smoke or the water with filth. . . ." J. S. Mill had argued before him against the gospel of economic growth, declaring that "a stationary state of capital and population implies no stationary state of human improvement. There would be as much scope as ever for all kinds of mental culture, and moral and social progress; as much room for improving the art of living, and much more likelihood of its being improved, when minds ceased to be engrossed by the art of getting on.") Nor is the story different on the continent. The sober-eyed injunction to know one's cultural inheritance and distrust it, to fight free of it, to seek some original encounter with experience, sloughing off bourgeois and other forms, has been the staple stuff of existential thought from its beginnings. "You must change your life," cries the poet Rilke—and the command has now become the keyword of the party of survival.

But obeying it means suffering, as has begun to be widely understood. Steadily, ever more clearly, men are coming to grasp that what they were doing was wrong, that what they have been, they must now begin to cease to be, that what their children are to become cannot flow from what they, the parents, have set before them as The Good, and that in discontinuity and interruption lies not disaster but the single ground of a habitable future. These new understandings link up, in psychological terms, with those inspired by the other major domestic event of this age—the discovery of the black experience. The latter discovery raised the question whether the obliviousness of our fathers to the suffering and inhumanity endured by millions of black men in their midst did not invalidate history, precedent, and "accepted moral tradition" as guides to behavior. Who could believe in the significance or dignity of such an uncaring past?

And the impact of the discovery of the abuse of nature—the ecological crisis—is to intensify that question, while extending the area of doubt from history to the self. For the crisis of survival doesn't simply call into question once more the worth of respected institutions, or the shibboleth of success, or the bootstrap myth, or the sanctity of abundance, technological revolution, "labor-saving devices," automation, "economic expansionism," and the rest. It challenges the conception of personal development and self-realization that has governed Western culture for centuries, established its sense of public and private priorities, provided its clearest definitions of crime and of virtue, taught it the terms on which history can be regarded as purposeful.

What will come of this challenge? It will either attain full potency, some say, ultimately interposing a barrier between space-ship Earth and those forces of ego-ridden greed that have willed a "world wasteland"—or it will be overmatched, borne down by the counterpressures of social myth and habit: in the balance of the contest hangs survival. Impressive and believable as this account of our situation is, it's hardly an adequate guide to the human realities lying just ahead. What it cannot body forth is the character of that inner human experience—the quality of the new self—upon which hope now rests. It is one thing to say we must learn to "doubt our values," strive to become critical of our culture, and another to imagine the desiderated state of mind from within. We are asked, in the name of survival, to become our own witnesses, to see ourselves from outside, to turn against "bourgeois values," to sit like Harry Haller in Hesse's story of a lone wolf and gaze down the stairs at the neat plants in our mid-dle-class hallways, at our cleanliness, our dutifulness, our high-gloss responsibility, our rectitude as hitherto understood—we are asked to gaze at all this and read it finally as error and deceit and corruption. ("Nobody has solved the problem," says Professor Boulding, "of how to prevent the insidious corruption both of the culture of the powerful and the culture of the impotent.")

Our task, we're told, is to teach ourselves to become, man by man, woman by woman, each the agent of his own disman-tling—his own movement on from a received "cultural self" to an unknown new identity. Against the greed that chokes our air we're to pit the prod of self-analysis, but not the hope of self-approval, the untender energies of self-critique, but not the fan-tasies of reconciliation. *For what we have been we must now cease to be.* Nearly twenty years ago Lewis Mumford saw in prospect "the joining, in intimate partnership, of the automaton and the id, the id rising from the lower depths of the unconscious, and the automaton, the machine-like thinker and the manlike machine, wholly detached from other life-maintaining functions and human reactions, descending from the heights of conscious thought. The first force has proved more brutal, when released from the whole personality, than the most savage of beasts; the other force, so impervious to human emotions, human anxieties, human purposes, so committed to answering only the limited range of questions for which its apparatus was originally loaded, that it lacks the saving intelligence to turn off its own compulsive mechanism, even though it is pushing science as well as civilization to its own doom." And, given the correctness of the prophecy, at least as assumed by the ecological spokesmen, there appears no alternative save that of extricating ourselves from our past, bending ourselves totally to an act of dissociation, laboring after intensities of self-consciousness that alone can dissolve the unifying cultural myths and symbols of an age.

It is precisely here—in the command to uncreate ourselves—that the deepest cultural meanings of the ecological cause come into view. Presented with a new mode of Apocalypse, we are to grasp that the quest for the freedom of love, the dream of full self-acceptance—release from the experience of self-rejection, self-repudiation, self-contempt—is no longer affordable. And there is no turning to nature, fierce nature or kind, for help, in the manner of Randall Jarrell's woman at the zoo who sought aid from a vulture ("You know what I was/You see what I am: change me, change me!") There is no turning anywhere outside the self. Salvation as alienation, complacency as suicide, security as self-doubt: our new Tablet, our new laws of personal balance and wholeness, are rigorously self-made. The claims implicit in the ecological rhetoric may or may not deserve condescension, skepticism, the distaste civilized minds reserve for melodrama. But it's clear even now that no small part of their meaning, in people's inward lives, lies in the truth that even in the act of disbelieving them, men near their own borders, approach perhaps the severest tests yet known of human nerve.

Mod Wishbook

Need a rucksack or some Kaibab boots? Plans for a log cabin or a Fuller sun dome? How-to books about carpentry, wiring, plumbing, furniture building, farming, weaving, home medicine, knitting? Want to buy a soil test kit, a loom, a kiln, seeds, bulk food, hand mills, solar stills, other items useful in starting a new world? The place to turn if you're in these markets is the *Whole Earth Catalogue—Access To Tools,* published by the non-profit Portola Institute of Menlo Park, California. And even if your needs are different, it won't hurt to imagine yourself as a *Whole Earth* sort of consumer. For in addition to being the first wishbook of its kind in history, the *Catalogue* is rich in revelation of national character. And unlike the competition—Sears, Monkey Ward and the rest—it's tight at the edge of Now.

Character revelation and Now-mongering aren't, to be sure, the Whole Earth gang's prime bag. (The key man in the bag is a young Stanford science graduate named Stewart Brand, who spent $40,000 of his own, his parents' and his grandparents' money before seeing his project begin to earn out.) The original aim was merely to list and describe, in a semiannual publication, every known item purchasable in the USA that's "useful as [a] tool," "relevant to independent education," notable for "high quality or low cost," and easily available by mail. And if the competition bug ever does bite the creators, it's plain their first move will have to be to scrap their format. For, viewed from a design standpoint, these 128 *Life*-sized pages qualify as some kind of minor disaster. The organization is haphazard (items are switched from sensible categories to silly ones "because this was a spare page"), the spelling is weird (*wierd, indispensible,* etc.), the makeup is confusing (hard to tell which copy goes with which picture), and the typography breaks the brain (with *Whole Earth* letter sizes you could print *Moby Dick* on a green stamp and sell space).

But, given the creators' aspirations as of this moment, the unsightliness doesn't matter. What counts, as indicated, is the *Catalogue*'s performance as a witness to the age. Profs and pundits (present writer guilty, of course) fret and agonize about where we're at, where we're headed, what it all means; this *Catalogue* acts. It defines significant contemporary longings, tells how to meet them, and in the process bodies forth the central assumptions of a putative new world in the making. One of these assumptions is that, because of the choking pollutions of technology and bigness, it's time the whole country went on a back-to-nature, do-it-yourself trip—rediscovered how to meet basic human needs without help from industry. (Hence the cabin plans and the handyman books.) Another assumption is that "basic human needs" include knowledge and art, and that nothing is more self-improving than meeting these needs by personal effort. (Hence the *Catalogue* lists hundreds of learning aids for self-propelled students of everything from geometry to Yoga, basketry to psychedelics, guitar to glassblowing.)

Still another assumption is that true self-sufficiency requires, if not social revolution, then an enormous increase in "intentional communities" whose members march to drums unheard in ordinary American towns. (Hence the *Catalogue* offers an index of practical and theoretical advice on a variety of modes of community development—selections and summaries of books by Buckminster Fuller, Marshall McLuhan, Paul Goodman, surveys of government publications detailing the expertise of community workers in the Peace Corps, Vista and elsewhere, and much more.)

Admittedly, assumptions like these sound undramatic—the chance seems slim that mere shopping lists and product descriptions could enliven them. But the *Whole Earth Catalogue* is in fact an uncommonly exciting read. Browsing in these pages fills the head with fantasies of independence and imagined joys of provisioning—a sort of Crusoe experience. ("On a tramp through the fields and forests," the *Catalogue* quotes deliciously from a work on wild mushrooms, "carry with you a small jar of butter, creamed with salt and pepper. On finding any edible mushroom —except morels or elfinsaddles—collect a few dry sticks and fire them. Split a green stick—alder or willow—at one end. Put the mushroom in the cleft, hold it over the fire until tender, season with the butter. Eat from the stick.") And the impatient, pressing, activist voices that review and ruminate on the listed goods and services awake forgotten energies and appetites inside the reader. Here and there the activism in question spreads itself out in rhetorical, self-conscious gestures. The editors maunder on at one point about "a realm of intimate, personal power [that] is developing—power of the individual to conduct his own education, find his own inspiration, shape his own environment, and share his adventure with whoever is interested."

But more often they simply do their thing—meaning they react and speak in ways that reveal a fine relish of human responsiveness and variousness. Locked-in selves, single visions, one-sideness—again and again these draw hostile comment. ("I only wish," says the *Whole Earth* review of *Consumer's Guide*, "that [they'd] print ads, give the manufacturers a place to beef back, liven up the Liberal Hour.") And again and again the editors hector their audience to resist the forces that shut men into the jail of routine and habit. ". . . Practice delaying the habitual, automatic and unthinking response," says the reviewer of Maxwell Maltz's *Psycho-Cybernetics,* picking up the quote from the text. Notice the difference (says the reviewer of a book on brain functions), notice the difference between the closed-in, "juvenile," hence "self-opinionated" cerebral cortex, and man's "perceptual system"—a nobler contrivance because more flexible, "more active, [more] intellectually honest in refusing to stick with one of many possible solutions." Study Bucky Fuller, attend to the true gospel of self-reliance—the word that challenges men to put aside "everything but your own experience," and build a faith on that. Heed the inventors of alternative lifestyles —"suburban guerrillas," as one reviewer calls them, in a passage that embodies the core of the *Catalogue* "philosophy:"

> Someday, after I've lived in the suburbs longer, I'd like to write an essay about my vision of the suburban guerrilla. He's a definite phenomenon. There's a sizeable [sic] population of them here in the San Francisco Bay area, men and women out to enjoy the advantages of town life without paying the customary penalties. Every suburban guerrilla probably has his own definition of himself, but my own sense of him is this: he has a job, but not a career. He likes the comforts, but doesn't want to go into debt for them. He makes distinctions between things that are good and things that are merely expensive. He may go in for elegance, or he may dig the funky scene. Hippies, after all, are urban guerrillas. But hippies are kids mainly grooving on each other in special enclaves, and that isn't quite what I'm talking about. I'm talking about people who see the possibility of a rich and abundant adult life within the context of those same suburban communities generally condemned as such hopeless wastelands that "real" life cannot be supported there. The suburban guerrilla I have in mind is of the suburbs, as well as *in* them.
>
> He challenges the assumption that the suburban context is hard, absolute, impenetrable, like plastic. To him, more like a piece of cheesecloth, full of holes to breathe through, and to wind in and out of, like a morning glory, or a pole bean. He borrows much of his point of view from the orientals. He realizes that life goes on in the suburbs just like every other place, even if most of the people there are too blind and deaf to see and hear it. The guerrilla lives by his wits, one day at a time. This makes him alert and alive. He has a talent for cultivating the holes in his cheesecloth. One hole might simply be the way the world is at six A.M. Another might be firsthand knowledge of all the footpaths in the neighborhood. He creates his freedom here and there and now and then, and by diligence winds up with as much as any conscious man anywhere. His landscape is small and patterned, but there are discoveries to be made on it, discoveries that can feed his own life at the same time they are important to the culture. I know of one elderly couple that subsists almost

entirely on the food they raise in their organic garden in the backyard of their home in suburban Menlo Park. As far as I'm concerned, the trip those two people are on, the life they are proving possible, is the most inspiring radical activity in all of San Francisco's radical environs.

Everywhere, in sum, the *Catalogue* comes on not as mere rustic hucksterism, but as a revivifier of faith in the human capacity to fight through to personal freedom regardless of layerings of environment, job, social situation, cultural or historical conditioning. And the cumulative effect is exhilarating: in place of whining, goldbricking, pot-light, doomed youth, as conjured up in a thousand solemn editorials, a different generation materializes—one that's come to work as well as play, one that means above all to own its own life.

Are there absurdities in this wishbook? Dozens. Many do-it-yourself activities that are cried up are cute or worse. (Each book listed is reviewed by an enthusiast; the enthusiasms include gathering salad greens in Central Park, cooking macrobiotically, turning on with or without drugs.) Some products described are jokes that don't come off—Boffers, for instance, $11 foam rubber swords described as "the first significant advance in weaponry since the encounter group." Others, like the Moog Synthesizer ($3500–8000) are kind of hard to park in the tipi. The evaluations of certain intellectual heroes, furthermore—John Cage and Arthur Koestler in particular—are in parts naïve, loony, or both. The obvious orientation in many sections of the *Catalogue* is toward commune people. (Stewart Brand and his wife lived for a time in a Bay Area commune, and once traveled about among California communards with a truck store, peddling books, tools and other materials to this growing market.) And that breed is romanticized throughout—not a hint of its Spahn Ranch dimensions.

But despite many faults and much nonsense, the *Catalogue* remains an extremely useful object. The alternative world it creates is deeply Californian, sometimes mindless, and can't possibly nourish all the illusions it generates. But it's on the side of life and purpose, and thinking about it even at a distance is a downright heartening trip.

Beyond the Ratrace:
The First Metamorphics
and the Quest for a New Gospel
(a fragment of cultural history)

—Turning and turning, a puzzle no less to themselves than to their elders, the new youth were clearly contemptuous of old metaphors, had formed a habit actually of spitting at their pretensions, and could not be taught to stand still. "The ratrace," "making it," "the bitch goddess," "the competitive way of life," success, failure, *The Rise of Silas Lapham, The Rise of David Levinsky,* at length (at mid-century) *The Man in the Gray Flannel Suit* Declining the Top Job—these icons and symbols, trivial or exotic to our ears, had been compelling figures for generations, holding fluidities of dailiness in a vessel of pseudo-understanding, providing evaluative measures for experience, determining the texture of imaginations, molding contours of hope. That the myths and figures mentioned were anti-human and perfunctory is demonstrable. Yet no less demonstrable is that their grip upon life (when God died *they* survived) was wonderfully intense. In a word, the moment of their own passing—we may safely date it after mid-century—was, for the elders of an entire culture, eerie, fearful, grave.

For a time, inevitably, the decline in symbolic authority went unacknowledged: revolution is not ingested overnight. A debate raged, in magazines and books, on television and lecture platforms and during election campaigns, as to whether major changes truly were in progress. What could be more probable, said some, than that exploiters and commercialists were attempting to create a "revolutionary youth" out of the void, for vulgar purposes of profit? A pollster, Samuel Lubell, reported that "only 10 percent" of his interviewees saw the work-world differently from their parents. A California sociologist pronounced that in his area 400 out of 500 youngsters thought well of the elders. A psychologist at Michigan University, Joseph Adelson, argued that talk of a break in continuity was extravagant, and attributed its prevalence to "essays on youth" in quality magazines:

> Not too surprisingly perhaps [wrote Adelson, confidently] the most likely writer of these essays is an academic intellectual, teaching humanities or the social sciences in an elite university. Hence he is exposed, in his office, in his classes, to far more than the usual number of radical or hippyesque students. (And he will live in a neighborhod where many of the young adolescents are preparing themselves for such roles.) On top of this, he is, like the rest of us, subject to the common errors of social perception . . .

But the comfort derived from such voices was of short duration, for those whose family lives had been touched by change demanded the right (in the contemporary phrase) to enter the dialogue. The magazine *Fortune* published a poll contradicting the conclusions of Lubell. The celebrated anthropologist Margaret Mead set her weight behind the thesis that the new youth were "like the first generation born in a new country," that they were in rebellion "all around the world, rebelling against whatever forms the governmental and educational systems take," and that the "deep, new, unprecedented, worldwide generation gap" was in no sense whatever fictive.

Few forces were more influential in shortening the debate in question than the media. Its attentiveness to the emergent sensibility was unrelenting; it soon put beyond doubt that a trans-

formation was occurring; its doggedness provided later generations with all that was to be known of The Early Ones, *ur*-
Metamorphics whose example still speaks so tellingly.* As every
schoolboy knows, it was during Richard Nixon's first White
House term, in the pages of a business paper, the *Wall Street
Journal*, that the first reports of The Early Ones appeared. Col-
lege-trained Youth Shun the Professions for Free Form Life,
said the headline above an account of Primitive Metamorphic
Lifestyle. A San Francisco Sextuple Darter named John Spitzer
in his twenties (cabdriver/bartender/magazine editor/Harvard
summa cum laude/pianist/playwright) revealed that he was con-
templating Septenary—a position as disk jockey. A second Early
One, Clara Parkinson, proved to be a Fem Tyrowhirler. Clara
had majored in government at Smith College, graduating in
1968, and thereafter taken up work as a letter carrier, because
impelled to "get off the treadmill." "I've discovered," said the
pioneer Tyrowhirler, in terms that may have stirred dread in contemporary readers' minds, "I've discovered a new sense of my
physical strength from lifting mail sacks." And a third Early One
was the Trimorph Chip Oliver (professional footballist/guru/
cook) whose word for the press was that he had never felt "more
together," and that he had lost a lot of weight ("50 pounds from
his playing weight of 230").

To speak of one or another of The Early Ones as having
"stirred dread" is, of course, speculative. (The present writer, a
Dimorph whirled only recently from Playfiction to Playhistory,
wishes to note here that he has already learned that few tasks
are harder for the historian than that of imagining the familiar
as it seemed to men when it was strange. More of this shortly.)
But it does seem clear that attention wasn't long diverted from
"the decline of the ratrace." It seems equally clear that the first
efforts to confront transformation were couched in moral vocabu-
laries—assessments of the ethics of "dropping out." And it is no
less certain that the preeminent moralists of the period were
those of the Yale School.

---

* The term Metamorphic had interesting origins. The earliest recorded
use we find occurs in a campaign speech delivered in 1976 by the last
presidential candidate to run under the standard of the Republican political
party—Spiro Agnew. The exact phrase was: "muddled meddling Metamorphics."

Nervous, ill-informed, beamish, lacking in analytical foundation, the Yale School was nevertheless highly advanced for its time, and, in collaboration with the media, played no small role in releasing the public from bondage to the fantasy that human nature would everywhere and always be the same. The chief spokesmen for the School were the novelist-youth authority-undergraduate counselor, John Hersey, Charles Reich, a Professor of Law, and Kenneth Keniston, a psychologist. All three laid it down that the rejection of "ratracing" or competition signified the advent of a higher moral consciousness, a new goodness, possibly the long-heralded perfection of the race. Hersey considered that the new youth had committed itself to a war on greed:

> Relating and helping are more important than making it. . . . "Relating" really means being able to give and take. The impulse to give, in a time when there is so much misery and pain at large, is very strong and takes many forms, from the handing out of oranges to total strangers at the Woodstock rock festival [a contemporary saturnalia], to the fevered, devoted work a Peace Corps volunteer may undertake. . . . Each young person in his way has had his urge to do *something* to make the world a better place. . . . The vast majority of young people believe that greed is at the root of most of the misery of the world, and that most businesses systematize greed. (*Letter to The Alumni*, 1970)

Reich concurred, expressing similar notions as follows:

> Consciousness III [a name for New Youth] does not think much of fighting for change from the comfort of personal security and elegance. He feels that if he is to be true to himself he must respond *with* himself. . . . He may take a job teaching in a ghetto school, which offers neither prestige nor comfort but offers the satisfaction of personal contact with ghetto children. He does not assume that he can fight society while luxuriating in its benefits. He must take risks—the risk of economic loss, of discomfort, of physical injury, of a jail sentence. . . . Consciousness III is . . . seeking to replace the infantile and destructive self-seeking that we laud as "competition" by a new capacity for working and living together. (*The Greening of America*, 1970)

And Keniston declared that young people were "taking the highest . values" for their own, internalizing and identifying these values "with their best selves," and struggling "to implement them."

As would be guessed, youth was not averse to learning of the achievement, by it, of moral distinction superior to that hitherto known. When, for example, the business paper quoted above asked Trimorph Chip Oliver about the moral dimensions of his dartings, this Early One slipped comfortably into self-congratulation:

> We're putting on a demonstration. . . . We're showing people a new way of life. We're showing people that as soon as you start loving and relating to people you'll find those people loving and relating to you.
>
> (*Wall Street Journal,* June 24, 1970)

And it can be imagined that parents were heartened by his words: was not (if a small joke may be ventured) was not Chip off the old block?

But dourer voices—knockers not boosters—demanded hearings. Reviewers and commentators took exception to Charles Reich's *The Greening of America,* objecting to the book's thesis that the young truly cared about others (an acerb *New York Times* writer named Lehmann-Haupt proposed the young were in love with their boots). The sociologist Edward Shils, writing in chilly tones in the English journal *Encounter,* doubted the *content* of the new morality: these children, said Shils, discover nothing but "the vacuum of the expanding and the contentless self." Bruno Bettelheim, the psychologist, spoke fiercely against children "fixated at the temper tantrum stage."

Within months, furor about the Metamorphics' virtue (or lack of it) filled the press. An account of the moralized justifications, apologia, attacks and counterattacks of the sixties and seventies—a survey of the Byzantine complications of casuistry on such matters as "arrogance" and "nihilism" vs. "frankness" and "freshness"—is beyond the compass of a short monograph. We cannot begin to suggest the range of obsessions that seized those resolved in this period to be "fair to youth." Observer after observer—artists, social scientists, politicos—was waylaid by trivia, edged off from sustained, penetrating study of the new behavior, by marginal if furiously argued considerations. There was—choosing one example at random—the Costume Issue. What was the meaning (so ran the momentous query) of the Metamorphics' dress code? The Yale School's Charles Reich found the clothes redolent of ethical significance:

> The new clothes express profoundly democratic values. There are no distinctions of wealth or status, no elitism; people confront each other shorn of these distinctions . . . [The old clothes] spoke of competition, advantage, and disadvantage. The new clothes deny the importance of hierarchy, status, authority, position, and they reject competition. . . .

Others found the clothes merely redolent. The novelist Saul Bellow affirmed, in *Mr. Sammler's Planet* (1970), that the new costume constituted a descent into chaos and self-destruction:

> What one sees on Broadway while bound for the bus. All human types reproduced, the barbarian, Redskin, or Fiji, the dandy, the buffalo hunter, the desperado, the queer, the sexual fantasist, the squaw, bluestocking, princess, poet, painter, prospector, troubadour, guerrilla, Che Guevara, the new Thomas Becket . . . Just look [at this] imitative anarchy of the streets—these Chinese revolutionary tunics, these babes in unisex toyland, these surrealist warchiefs, Western stagecoach drivers—Ph.D.s in philosophy, some of them . . . They sought originality. They were obviously derivative. And of what—of Paiutes, of Fidel Castro? No, of Hollywood extras. Acting mythic. Casting themselves into chaos . . .

The critic John Aldridge construed the costume as a badge of banality:

> . . . the U.S. army tunics of World War I . . . the broad-brimmed hats and plunging sideburns of the Western plainsman . . . the headbands of Comanche braves . . . Edwardian suits, the smocks of French Bohemian painters, or the gaudy saris of guruland . . . The young need to have something to do with their banality . . . (*In the Country of the Young*, 1970)

Scores of other opinions were sternly set down.

Or consider the battle about sexuality. Did the Metamorphics intend to banish Masculinity? Would Matriarchy come again? A sleuth known for probes of homosexuality in classic American fiction, Leslie Fiedler, looked warily at "The New Mutants" (1966) for evidence of the feminization of culture. A psychologist, Karl Stern, took up cudgels on the other side, in a work called *The Flight From Woman* (1966), hinting that any weakening of competitive energies might mean a coming-to-terms at last with the long-suppressed femininity of the male psyche itself: all hail an imminent reign of tenderness. Everywhere, as it seemed, intellect drove itself toward the peripheral, the inessential, the sensational, the reductive—with the result that, as at many an earlier moment in human history when breath has departed a ruling myth, and the path ahead is darkness, confusion and distraction mounted.

And at length were overcome. That latter part of our story —the brilliant *fin de siècle* effort at reconstruction—has been well told elsewhere. Heroic names and achievements have been recorded; the classic texts have had their scrupulous exegetes; minor technical problems alone remain. One further word may be said here, though, toward the end of dispelling the impression, rather widespread just now, that the age we survey was in every intellectual quarter inane. Granted, a backward glance over those troops of self-important, preening "youth authorities," pundits, moralists, social science "experts," cynical political revivifiers (on the Right) of a dying Superego—granted that such a backward glance gives small encouragement to the belief that the age knew any growing points save the Early Metamorphics themselves. Granted too that, with the quality of the general mind of the day firmly before us, it seems likely that the Early Ones' refusal to articulate a program, their preference for doing it rather than saying it, was at bottom a response to the lambent dullness roundabout. Amid so much muck, madness, nonsense and false piety, who could possibly have grasped the truth?

Yet while impatience with the age is understandable, it is not altogether just. The language we now speak, the conceptual schemes on which we now rest, were—true enough—little dreamed of then. Dartings, whirlings, substitute lateral gratification, Possibilitarianism, the movement from Tyrowhirler to Septenary and on across the band toward Life-Exhaustion—few could have comprehended the bearings of these terms. Our commonplaces—awareness that lifemeaning resides wholly in the exploration of human possibility, in the process of multiple selfcreation, not in any goals, results or consequences—our commitment to the maintenance of open-mindedness and universal Playwork Participation in all public and private roles—these commonplaces of our times have no precise counterparts in late twentieth-century thought.

Yet from this it does not follow that the period must be dismissed out of hand as a blank. Calling the roll of the insightful of those times is saddening: some voices have been lost, and none that survives achieved lifecontact with The Early Ones themselves. Still a few of these minds matter. One notable, if abstract, formulation of proteanism appeared in the mid-sixties, for instance, in a foundation-supported journal called *Daedalus*. The formulator was a young political scientist, G. Kateb by name, who wrote as follows:

> We have . . . referred to the utopian possibility of making life as as a whole "more plastic." What we mean to suggest by these phrases is the allowance for a greater relaxation in the definitions of self, role, vocation, than the world customarily allows. Proteus could become the symbol of the tone of utopian life. The aim would be to encourage self-expression to the point where the traditional boundaries between fantasy and reality would become more blurred, to allow individuals to assume various "personae" without fear of social penalty, to allow groups to come together and affect diverse communal relations and then disband, to allow for the greatest possible accumulation of vicarious, mimetic, or semi-genuine experience, to strive to have each self be able to say, in the words of Walt Whitman's "Song of Myself," "I am large, I contain multitudes," and, finally, in the name of heightened consciousness and amplitude of being to diminish the force of the duality of male and female. And for this "playing at life" to take worthwhile forms and conclude in splendid enrichment of character, the mind and feelings must be cultivated, the capacity to experience the higher pleasures must be developed, the higher faculties must be in control. Otherwise the playing at life would remain just that, and not be, instead, an instrument of self-transcendence. ("Utopia and the Good Life," 1965)

The strongest work of the period, however, was that of the still-remembered Henry S. Kariel. It was Kariel who, in *The Promise of Politics* (1966), drew attention to metamorphic, self-exploratory, non-authoritarian dimensions of "such disparate personalities as Socrates, Diogenes, Montaigne, Voltaire, Franklin, Henry Adams, Brecht, and Kennedy, and . . . Don Quixote and Huck Finn," and who delivered, in a remarkable chapter entitled "Man in Process," a virtual prophecy of the present age:

In this . . . newly framed picture, man may be seen as an elusive, incomplete being forever in the process of self-discovery and self-development. He is pre-eminently an innovating creature. In the concise terms of Christian Bay, he is "free to the extent that he has the *capacity, the opportunity,* and the *incentive* to give expression to what is in him and to develop his potentialities." There is no effort here to fill in what he is to be free *for*. He is simply free from those self-mutilating traits that produce the mindless fanatic, enthusiast, or nihilist, that keep him from acknowledging and developing himself. In the language of Marx, he is free "to do one thing today and another tomorrow, to hunt in the morning, fish in the afternoon, rear cattle in the evening, criticize after dinner." He is free to play these roles, Marx significantly added, "without ever *becoming* hunter, fisherman, shepherd, or critic." . . . He is a probing, experimenting being, always in motion, attaching and detaching values, inflating and deflating alternatives, unsure of his place in the order of things, skeptical and above all, aware of his skepticism.

Kariel moved on from these themes to the greater issues, in *Open Systems: Arenas for Political Action* (1968)—even coming to face the question that has preoccupied our own century: "How open an area for protean action can we contemplate?" In a most moving preface to the latter work, he speaks of the gulf separating him from The Early Ones, both Primitive Metamorphics like Clara and Chip and John, and the Great Early One, Jerry Rubin himself:

> . . . I also know there are roles I *could* play [Kariel writes wanly] . . . There are a great many . . . roles I can conceive of myself playing. And yet, it is obvious to me, I fail to play them. I do not travel readily or lightly. Not for me Ishmael's voyage. I am tenured, committed, identified, defined. I still have various options—not playing Ahab, to be sure, but possibly Ishmael. Yet I fail to exercise them. I am aware not only of being limited (which no longer depresses me) but of being *needlessly* limited. I *could* without damage to myself test more possibilities and be at least somewhat more playful. I could play more parts, participate more. Nevertheless, here I am, voluntarily limited and enclosed.

Who among us, reading these sentences, can fail to be touched by the pathos of this address, and by the implicit difficulty of the struggle in those years to Break Free? And who among us can be unmoved by the tale of Kariel's neglect in his own time? His pioneering essays rationalizing the Metamorphics as "proto-types of the open-ended personality system" were printed in literary reviews with subscription lists of a few thousand. None of the great university presses or trade publishers of the period undertook to bring out his pioneering volumes on enlarging experiential range, or those works contending that men "must test the degree of *tolerable* disruption," that politics must be injected into all closed systems, that men must *pry open* their personality systems, their science and knowledge systems, their social systems, and that the aim of life is to *disrupt imposed experiences*. (The seminal volume, *Open Systems,* was brought out in a tiny unnoticed edition by Loyola University Press.) Kariel held no honored chair in his teaching lifetime (much of his career was spent at the University of Hawaii!), and the bibliographies of that age, which show endless special issues and festschrifts for Herman Marcuse, Norbert O. Brown, Newton Mailer and others equally obscure, reveal no interest in his name. Even within his own profession, when his themes were glancingly touched upon—process orientation, for instance, or the protean psychological style (see an essay published in 1967 called "Protean Man" by a professor named Robert Lifton), Kariel's name went unmentioned. The clear case is that the quest for the new gospel began in his pages, and the story of his neglect is truly depressing.

Were there others? A few. None of their writing has the force of the classic texts, to be sure. None matches, say, those extraordinary paeans to self-disorientation found in Jerry's touchstone parable of the Yippies freaking the college newspaper editors:

> the room echoed with hysterical screams. "Stop it! Stop it! Stop it!" A voice boomed over a bullhorn: "Attention! This is Sergeant Haggerty of the Washington Police. These films were smuggled illegally into the country from North Vietnam. We have confiscated them and arrested the people who are responsible. Now clear this room! Anyone still here in two minutes will be arrested!"
>
> The editors fell over themselves rushing for the door. People were trampled. Noses bloodied. Clothes ripped to shreds . . . A husky crewcut cat, in suit and tie . . . climbed up on a chair

and yelled, "I've just come back from Vietnam. My brothers died in my arms. The fools in the White House are going to kill us all. We are college editors. We have power. We must be brave!"

Is this guy real? Or part of the Washington Theater group? I didn't know. But did it make any difference. Everything was *real* and *unreal*. The editors were stunned. Chaos and anarchy reigned. . . . "You will have to decide for yourself whether the police are real or not." . . . People broke down, crying . . . They began talking to one another . . . It was an emotional breakthrough. Through theater they learned something about themselves.

Such words do not abide our question.

Yet on occasion the cause of disorientation, and of movement through roles, was articulated, even this early, in terms of specific changes in public servants and public policy. An urban planner, Richard Sennett, argued—in a work called *The Uses of Disorder* (1970)—that people of his profession victimized themselves and others by over-rigid self-definitions. Sennett compared the city planners to certain overprotective young doctors:

> . . . these young doctors have . . . a peculiar kind of strength—a power to cut themselves off from the world around them, to make themselves distant, and perhaps lonely, by defining themselves in a rigid way. This fixed self-definition gives them a strong weapon against the outside world. . . . The threat of being overwhelmed by difficult social interactions is dealt with by fixing a self-image *in advance*, by making oneself a fixed object rather than an open person liable to be touched by a social situation.

Sennett argued that the same rigidity afflicted planners, and that it must be overcome, for, as he declared:

> This attitude is a way of denying the idea of history, i.e., that a society will come to be different than it expected to be in the past. In this way, a planner at his desk can steel himself against the unknown outside world in the same way that a young doctor steels himself against his fear about the experience of dealing with his patients. . . .

And in 1970 a striking paper was read to the Committee on Social Stratification and Social Mobility of the Seventh World Congress of Sociology at Varma, Bulgaria. Entitled "Strategies for Social Mobility," it was the work of two scholars—S. M. Miller of New York University and Pamela Roby of George Washington University—who acknowledged uncompromisingly that the metaphor of the rise had lost substance for the commonality. Better henceforth, they proposed, to imagine mobility as a progress through various kinds of work, not as linear upward movement in a particular organization. "Higher and lower positions are not so much the issue," they opined; the crux is movement, change, variety, freshness. Theirs was, admittedly, a primitive effort. There was no hint of relish of Self-Whirl or Self-Explore in this paper. The motive was merely to patch up programs of compensatory education originally aimed at guaranteeing "upward mobility" to what were called "the disadvantaged." Yet, studied in its own context, it stands as a landmark.

And, as may as well be added, something of the same landmark quality attaches to the early commune-meditation centers. For invariably these institutes stressed rolevariousness in their programs—witness an advertisement for a center called CUMBRES, founded in 1970 at Dublin, New Hampshire:

> All permanent members of the staff share all the work. There is physical labor in gardening, maintaining the grounds, cleaning, preparing and serving food. There are creative and intellectual efforts in conducting seminars, leading groups, writing and designing brochures, coordinating programs, etc. There is spiritual work in study groups and in meditation. A member of the staff may be found preparing breakfast for the community in the morning, answering correspondence in the afternoon and leading a discussion group in the evening.

—But subtly, almost imperceptibly, the act of drawing together such documents teases us out of proportioned perception. We yield to the supposition that these documents were widely studied, that men "must have learned" from them the true character of the age struggling to birth. (Surely they knew as much by the beginning of the century's eighth decade—how else explain the quantity of evidence, as attested by our clusters of citations, bearing the date 1970?) Altogether easy for us to riffle through the museum of the past, collecting the prefiguring texts that have touched us, fashioned our being—great early works like Emerson's "Circles," key apothegms from "Self Reliance":

> When good is near you, when you have life in yourself, it is not by any known or accustomed way . . . —the way, the thought, the good shall be wholly strange and new.

Power ceases in the moment of repose, it resides in the moment of transition from a past to a new state, in the shooting of the gulf, in the darting to an aim.

How could process-orientation have remained a mystery?

But our question is, in the end, inadmissible. Right to speak flatly: what is obvious to us now—our way of reading the great texts, Marx, Sorel, Dewey, Bergson, Pirandello and the rest—was not obvious to them. Those who struggled, those who perceived the future and did not bog down in puerile squabbles about clothes or feminization or moral improvement or stabilization of egos, those who refused to meet the challenge of a dying age by scrambling back into the political rejuvenation of Superego—to these we owe full respect. They are our fathers, indeed our very selves.

But that such minds breathed—and were met with opprobrium or laughter—must not muffle our compassion for the others: even for the mockers themselves, the wholly blind. The historical hour they passed through had been traversed before. Serious disturbances had been known by their great-grandfathers, in the mid-nineteenth century, when the continuity of man and nature was disclosed, and again, two centuries earlier, when the planets were set in motion and poets shuddered:

> *Moving of th' earth brings harmes and feares,*
> *Men reckon what it did and meant—*

But the human fact is that the birth of the new is not made easier by memory of earlier births. The coming of an age when self too would "move," would seek endlessly, richly, appetitively the experience of transformation and metamorphosis: this was an eruption of terror like the quaking of planets. It cannot too often be repeated that for generations men had told each other the meaning of life lay not in the afterlife, not in the service of divinity, but in *work itself*, the struggle upward. "We must work!" cried Vershinin in Chekhov's *Three Sisters*. "There is nothing for us but work, all of us must work!"

And then all at once, as we have seen, work turned meaningless. Children shrugged, smiled condescendingly to their fathers. A university president of our period, Martin Meyerson, appears often to have repeated, in public speeches, the words of one of his students: "I know one thing, though. I know work isn't my thing. I do know work isn't my thing." Seemingly his tone was bemused—troubled but not hysterical. He doubtless hoped to allay fears of parents as he repeated the phrases, surrounding them with hopeful easing words. But it cannot have been easy for those listening then to hear life values lightly mocked. —My children won't work . . . But what then will they do? Who will discharge their obligations? How can society's labor be performed? How can human civilization be preserved? Are men to be orgiasts for life, grooving endlessly down the ringing grooves of change? People gazed into each other's eyes, frowning, looked away in fear. Old Scripture promised that "thy children shall return to thy borders"—but Old Scripture had no authority, and New Scripture was as yet unimaginable. Dismay, a steadily deepening sense of uselessness, worthlessness, purposelessness—the death of meaning . . . This was the experience, these were the torments. . . .

For us, thinking backward, penetrating the period imaginatively, perceiving the emotional excess of its depressions, reflecing on the ingenuity of our own open structures, our devices for non-violent testings of freedom, our marvelously flexible patterns of disruption, above all our opportunities for exhilarating lifetimes of self-whirling—for us the temptation is strong to consider that there is no lesson here save that of our superiority, our huge distance from their mean level of achievement. But here as elsewhere, as always for men, the truest lesson is the most compassionate. There is but one meaning in these years of quest and seeming defeat now far gone from living memory, that of human resiliency: the superb, *trustable* permanence of men's power—no matter what blankness oppresses our days—forever to renew and reconceive ourselves.

I Can't Sign:
Reflections of a "Moderate"

One Hundred on Columbia Faculty Urge
Strong Action to Halt [Class] Disrupters
—headline from *The New York Times*,
March 11, 1969

—End-of-summer picnic in a college town near Amherst. N., last seen in June, comes by with coffee and asks about the Columbia faculty unity statement—the one circulated by Trilling, Barzun and ninety-seven others last spring. Did the xerox he mailed ever arrive? What did I think? Spiky, distant, I back off, hide behind The Summer. I am depressed just by the reminder of that time—events at "our" college. "We" cooled a student strike into a "moratorium," then wrote a letter to Nixon explaining that our troubles were his fault, then lifted off on a great blown geyser of media approval and gamesmanly self-regard. —Too much going on, I say, summer committees, tons of mimeo stuff, I'd need to go back and reread the thing, awful memory . . . Did they have in mind circulating it, getting the Valley colleges to sign? (There are now five of us along the Connecticut River in western Massachusetts.) A steering committee? Thanks for the nudge, etc., send me the deadline, etc., sorry, etc., thanks again, etc.

This slipperiness smells—but what can you do? I remember the document perfectly—an expression of faculty solidarity in the face of student challenges—"attempts to disrupt or prevent the holding of classes." Doubtless the sponsors and signers shook hands all around in August, when the national student groups announced plans for fall hell weeks—the Chicago anti-war demonstration, the October shutdown by the Student Mobilization Committee, the first student strike, the first March on Washington. Members of the academic community, the statement said, must "accept their responsibility to protect each other's rights and demonstrate the will to act. . . . We call upon all members of this and other universities to defend by example and by action the fundamental principles of a free university. It is our intention not to surrender the safeguards of freedom that men have erected . . . over several centuries." The document actually came to me twice—first the xerox from N., and then the Columbia administration sent it out to alumni and friends, together with a long letter from the university president, saluting this "eloquent indication of faculty unity" and declaring that "a new spirit has been created on the campus in which the sharp and bitter divisions of last spring have disappeared."

It came in twice and in theory should have been welcome *chez moi*. A "moderate" statement, as they say—firm, not hysterical. A vote for the faculty interest that transcends individual campuses. A level of writing far above that of most faculty statement prose. (". . . The academic community is [not] supine or befuddled in the face of these challenges." Dean Barzun? "No genuine education can take place if teachers and students are cast in an adversary role." Professor Trilling?) No attempt to excuse complacency: the statement conceded the need for additional reforms in "university governance," an accompanying letter called for "more informed discussion and considered action . . . to remedy social ills and racial injustice, and to deal with the causes of war," and the text included an allusion to the possibility of faculty-student action in the area of curricular change.

And while part of my scratchiness about the document might

be laid to diffidence, reluctance to deliver another boring speech on a tattered subject, it wouldn't be a large part. For I'm not a true believer in diffidence in this context. I wince a lot, sure, beg to be spared—but I know people *ought* to talk up, even at the risk of tiresomeness. Many teachers' opinions about "disruption" are grainy, contradictory. The absence outside, among the general public, of any feeling for the graininess hurts. It also hurts inside. Uncertainty and ambiguity about individual faculty opinion are too often the rule: people can't grasp the next man's position, can't feel their way into its intricacies.

And once the crises arrive there's no time for full explanations. Heat's on, a run to moral stereotypes starts, ignorance feeds back. The White House announces that the wars of academe are between "moral arrogance" ,and cowardice, and overnight everybody's a figure in allegorical tableaux—flat-out face-offs of vice and virtue. Marcuseans call administrators cruel, sadistic repressors. Anti-Marcuseans yap at disrupters as egomaniacs and destroyers or hypocrites and traitors. Talks that begin with civil criticism of "egalitarians" or "elitists" zoom in a minute into damnation of monsters. If you're at University X and aware of the mimeo wars, you see that a famous colleague in the physical sciences is outraged about a proposal nobody proposed—he calls it "monstrous." ("It is monstrous to require professors of surgery to base the practice and teaching of their subject on a majority vote of the fourth-year medical students.") If you're at a faculty meeting at University Y, you hear a young assistant professor insisting that yesterday a faculty majority proved itself to be selfish, racist, in league with South Africa. (This was said after a tentative vote—reversed in a day or two—against admitting "underqualified Negroes.") The notion of being precise about who's fighting whom—or about what the opponents truly want—is thrown out as a trick, a strategy of delay.

—No, I believe (repeat) that people should spell themselves out. The only question is: Can a man represent himself fairly in quick party chat? At the picnic I doubted it. A minor qualm or two could have been shed—as, for example, that I was put off by the closed-in, on-this-rock-we-rest character of the Columbia statement. You are always looking for a sense of opening or exploration. You know why it's not there—Columbia has Had It—

but still it isn't there, and (sorry), not seeing it bugs me . . .
That's first and easiest. But as for the rest—

The rest takes more than a minute. The gist of it is this:
The avowed intent of the Columbia statement was to assert the
teacher's right to determine his subjects and modes of discourse
in accordance with his own best professional judgment—no inter-
ference, no bullying. But an indirect effect of the document was
to endorse the Class, the pure, undisruptable, sanctified MWF
11:00 A.M., as a quasi-"fundamental principle" in itself. Implicit in such endorsements is the suggestion that present faculty
differences about the uses of immediate experience in a teaching
/learning community (not to mention differences about whether
the right to dictate the terms of the learning situation must forever rest, non-negotiably, with the faculty) are a negligible item,
no barrier to unity. And that suggestion is wrong.

True enough, majority power still resides with the faction
that regards classes and courses and reported experience as the
only appropriate centers of intellectual activity in a university.
But a resistance movement does exist, and the developing struggle between the two forces needs to come farther into the open,
partly because it will help to revitalize and redefine the fundamental principles, partly because postponing an address to issues
of life-reference is likely to increase disruption instead of dimin-
ishing it.

Is my point over-obvious? If you bundle it into the too-
familiar bag with lectures about relevance and interdiscipline-
ism, of course it is. Once dumped there, it appears to be one more
manifestation of the new jockery or redskinism, one more adapta-
tion of the worn theme of education as moral self-improvement,
one more ground for rapping critics of the status quo as characters devoid of intellectual dignity. As every schoolboy knows,
rapping in that vein lately grows shriller. Across the field stretch-
ing from Jacques Barzun to Karl Shapiro to Edward Shils you
hear about "opportunists" or about grown men "sucking up to
the kids" or about over-permissivism and "treachery to the disciplines"—and about neurotics, new populists, library burners,
pro-illiterates, etc. Often the explicit charge is that the life-reference man is too ignorant to know the purposes served by dis-
tributing inquiry into manageable fields, by developing bodies of

knowledge transmittable in a classroom context. Repeatedly, teachers of substantial accomplishment find themselves obliged to swear their allegiance to high intellectual standards before they can go on to remind listeners that the artificiality of fields is too easily forgotten, and that the crucial need is for significant turnings-out from the controlled artificial environment of chair rows, blackboards, reported experience—the "discipline"—toward the texture of immediacy.

Fortunately, some teachers subject to this pressure aren't intimidated by it. The critic F. R. Leavis lectured a university audience quite untimidly a year or so ago on the wisdom of abolishing English courses that amount merely to some poems or novels or authors to be studied, or that fidget the term away with "practical criticism." The English teacher's proper concern, Leavis noted, is life itself—wrong to split it up or shave it down, wrong to leave it out (as many people do) "because 'it's not really real' or 'it's too important to matter.'" And with that concern in mind, he proposed a complete revision of the English major, looking toward a collaboration of teachers and students in day-to-day evaluation of contemporary communication, expression and personal life—a venture that would develop standards directly from the tension between lived life and literary versions of human creativity and social possibility, and that would not take the inviolable Class as its center.

And dozens of other teachers—"solid," well-respected professionals among them—continue to show comparable irreverence. A sociologist at the University of Pennsylvania—Rolf Meyersohn—publishes a critique of ordinary methods courses in his own subject. Why do teachers slight the truth that working sociologists use many other ways of testing and generating hypotheses besides desk-bound, digit-happy, Census Bureau interview and statistics methodology? Why ignore participant-observer techniques, attempts to learn about communities by studying the moment-to-moment effect of the investigator's own presence in the subject culture? How can justice be done to this kind of inquiry inside the classroom? . . . A maverick philosophy scholar at Queens College—John McDermott—publishes a fascinating study of American philosophical attitudes toward experience as a teacher. His pugnacious advice is that academic man try another look at Emerson, Dewey, James, Peirce—rediscover what was once made, in intellectual terms, of the method of experience, and perceive not merely the American-ness of the method, but its fruitfulness as well. ("Experience is our only teacher," says Peirce. How does learning occur with such a teacher? "It takes place by a series of surprises.") Should not schools institutionalize the dialectic between experience and disciplinary learning, work it into their deep structure?

There are, to be sure, difficulties and weaknesses on the life-reference or class-disrupting side. "We" are too sociable with the turn-on gang—drug cultists, sex experimenters, antinomians, mysticals, flamboyants, winners like the Wellesley lass at the last commencement who told the audience that she and her pals were out for ecstasy. (Go 'way, parents and teachers, you just can't understand.) And clear lines are rarely drawn—as should be done—between the cause of life-reference education, social revolution, social service, and pacifism.

But what matters is that many first-rate people in the academy—professionals who can't be dismissed as mollycoddlers, slobs, sentimentalists, political agitators, misplaced hipsters, hunters of lost youth—now understand that the key issue in academic confrontation concerns the proper relationship between the university and the edge of lived experience. Among these professionals a significant minority is bent, as indicated, on an indecorous gesture against the ancient, hallowed, reported-experience ground —as a way of seeking accreditation for immediate experience. And, owing to the nature of the times, the minority is gaining adherents. Events conspire, seemingly. Books like Moynihan's *Maximum Feasible Misunderstanding* showed readers the bad consequences of public policy that followed a "discipline version" of ghetto needs and ignored lived reality. The media that create "occasions" rather than art objects pull the culture ever more powerfully "into the act." Themes of anti-passivity pass into common parlance from existential writers . . . The lifestyle of unguardedness, downrightness, anti-decorum, involvement becomes a norm . . .

Would it not be better if the relevant pedagogical issues could be talked out on quiet turf, with no distractions? Certainly —but the circumstances of change can't always be nicely con-

trolled. Creating alternatives to traditional course patterns means
—as half a dozen new institutions have learned—inventing new
modes of collaborative planning between teachers and students,
new lines about admissions, evaluation, every aspect of conventional schooling. These aren't overnight jobs. They are, however,
substantial and decent jobs, and facing up to them is a prime
academic responsibility. It won't be seen as that, though, if the
life-reference cause is deprecated as with-it-ism or whimsy, or
smeared as a bullyboy threat to academic freedom. Somewhere
in the Columbia document—mainly in the stony, armored tones
of teacherly lordliness—I heard the old anti-experiential rag. And
it was from that that I backed off.

Well then, somebody says: What should we conclude? Academic freedom is nowhere endangered? Faculties haven't any
business insisting on their intellectual-pedagogical prerogatives?
No, that's not the claim. The claim—laying it out again—is that
faculty proclamations shouldn't, obliquely or otherwise, bless
pedagogical orthodoxy as the holystone of academic freedom.
What we want is something more spacious and realistic—an en-
dorsement of faculty rights that speaks to things as they are,
and eschews the Military Bit (EM there, officers here). Let faculty
statements begin with an admission that teachers aren't and can't
be and shouldn't be united in pedagogical theory at this moment.
Let them acknowledge that a fresh sense of university education
is in the air, posing more than a merely chichi challenge to established forms and procedures and assumptions. Let it be said
that there's an effort on the one hand to elevate the status of
immediate experience, to win acceptance for it as a genuine resource in higher learning. Give the petition-signers a chance to
say out loud that multi-track higher education—partly discipline-
oriented, partly experience-oriented—may well be a good thing;
that in schools to come the line between classroom and non-class-
room experience, intellectual and "merely personal" growth, may
be less boldy drawn; that we're not as certain as in yesteryear
that the conditions necessary and sufficient for a classroom to
become a place of learning are inviolability and teacher-domina-
tion; and that our former hierarchy of "places of learning" seems
just now rather shaky. (Nobody can learn to edit Persius by
living in a halfway house for adolescent delinquent boys; nobody

can assess the value of the concept of community, as Moynihan pointed out, merely by poring over Robert A. Nisbet and Paul Goodman in a library; nobody can confidently rank one activity higher than the other as an exercise of intellect.)

Let it be said, furthermore, that commonplace assumptions about the vast difference between teacher and student are also under current challenge as inimical to effective learning and teaching communities. Flexibility about status is found desirable by universities that are moving toward combinations of discipline-oriented and life-reference studies. For while the status of the teacher is unambiguous on the discipline-oriented side, elsewhere it's a different story, with tricky subplots. (Social service is one activity; development of self or identity is another; exploring connections between disciplinary models and the edge of experience is another.) There's an emerging tendency to link rights and powers in academic government with activities rather than with formal titles, and to vary policy concerning admissions, grading and the like in accordance with the character of specific teaching and learning enterprises. Where a firm discipline is being introduced, by teachers who are competent to represent it, to students who freely elect it, the undergraduate claim to the right to hire and fire continues to be seen as weak. Where no discipline, or only the beginning of a discipline exists, and reliance on experiential perception is necessary, the undergraduate claim to that right—and to the right of self-evaluation—is held to be stronger. (Harvard's faculty accepted this principle when it granted students a full vote on tenure appointments in its new black studies program.) The right would also be stronger in programs where the focus is on social service or on personal development than in programs where the turn to experience is directed along carefully judged disciplinary lines, and the student remains, unambiguously, a student.

Given the variety of the challenges to orthodoxy, the faculty statement might say, unqualified endorsements of any single existing pedagogical form conceivably could lock a university community into an unviable past. And, by the same token, persistence in speaking as though the barrier between teacher and student must everywhere and always remain absolute can intensify the difficulty of moving forward into a more variegated teaching world. But at the same time it *is* a fact that precisely because flexibility and an atmosphere of hospitality to experiment in teaching relationships are the order of the hour, some members of the university are encouraged to disruptive acts. They have violently interrupted discourse between students and teachers and done dirt on the ideal of rational inquiry. We call upon all members of the university community to stand firm against such behavior *without becoming standpatters*. The search for new terms of discourse and new forms of relatedness in higher education is an intellectual venture; it can't be pressed by mob action. Wherever it is so pressed, we shall oppose it with all our force. But our obligations can't be met merely by this act of resistance. We must proceed with the work of reconstituting teaching and learning relationships through reasoned, collaborative inquiry.

Ideally, a good law-and-order faculty document wouldn't stop here. It would go on to support its pieties about change, tolerance, openness to new pedagogy, with practical recommendations, some clear next steps to be taken by university communities. It could speak up, for instance, for an effort by student-faculty-administrator teams to identify teachers and advanced students whose research or teaching suggests sympathy with experientially-oriented pedagogy. (The results of the inventory could be used to shape proposals for restructuring in future years, to determine policy concerning faculty recruitment, and to guide thinking about the relative amounts of student "time" to be spent in orthodox courses and in a "school of immediate experience" in order to qualify for traditional degrees.) It could put an argument for an effort—by another team—to identify opportunities in the immediate environment (local government, business, agencies of welfare and of protest) for effective education, pointing outward from specific disciplines toward life situations. It could propose that the same teams accept responsibility for creating new agencies of communication within their institution (instruments for circulating news about ventures in life-oriented education already in progress), and for preparing rationales for multi-track higher education (in anticipation of times when the work of acquainting alumni and the public with its intricacies and value could begin), and for developing lines of communication with private employers (for the purpose of educating them in the value and uses of experiential programs that may or may not lead to traditional degrees), and for starting conversations with graduate school admissions committees, looking first toward the creation of fresh ways of evaluating applicants and later toward the encouragement of multi-track graduate education. ("Student movements focusing much of their aggression on their undergraduate experience are really protesting practices which are traceable to shortcomings in the graduate schools," says Professor Richard Worthen, concluding a research-in-teaching project for the Carnegie Corporation that took him to hundreds of campuses. "In the long run a thoroughgoing reform of the graduate departments of our universities is just about as important as a solution to our current Vietnam dilemma.")

—All this is airy, I admit. I should also admit, no doubt, that the notions presented here aren't presented as disinterestedly as they should be. A few weeks back I had my first fall term moment of confrontation—a hassle with the Class Clan. A new course I was offering was over-enrolled—one hundred and thirty-six names had signed on for a "seminar" in contemporary American cultural studies (limited to twenty students). Say everything you can think of against the enrollees: call them crazy mod-mad kids, abuse them for their boredom with the past, their lack of a sense of history, their absorption in NOW, etc. (No over-enrollment problems in my Shakespeare seminar.) Still, they thought they wanted—these children—to do some contemporary cultural studies; they signed up. During the summer, several wrote letters pressing their claims. And most of them didn't get a shot at what they wanted. I made a small effort, I say defensively. Before the term began I called the registrar, a helpful, giving man. I suggested that, after filling a seminar for myself, I might send off a letter to the rejected, including a complete list of other enrollees and saying that if anyone wished to start a seminar on his own, with advice from me on possible assignments, and with an off-campus focus, he should write at once or see me in my office. (I had in mind some journalistic assignments the results of which could be played off against the work of newspaper professionals, as well as against Mailer, Wolfe and others, with an eye to clarifying and criticizing certain contemporary conventions of reportage.)

The answer was: Please bring up the question of credit. Your letter should specify "on a no-credit basis." The vote was definite last spring: a student-run political thing was turned down in faculty meeting . . . I could go see the dean . . . Best to move slowly . . . If they really want it, they'll do it anyway . . . No need for credit . . . A class is a class. . . .

I admit this episode produced a patch of self-constriction and frustration and still colors my thoughts. I was itched by the stiffness that demanded absolute priority for the issue of credit. Up against the wall, kids. Frisk 'em, Mike. (Gotta watch these kids, they'll con you every time. . . .) Why couldn't we have started open and then closed in if they tried to con us? Why *begin* with a clanking gesture of suspicion?

But while this local exacerbation does stick in the memory, I wouldn't call it crucial. The arguments above are, after all, familiar, even commonplace; they don't need any particular person or situation to vouch for them. They amount at bottom to nothing more than (a) a plea for faculty credibility, and (b) a reiteration of the truism that academic freedom and obeisance to Standard-Current-Approved pedagogical forms aren't one and the same thing. The quite unradical (I think) assumption on which they rest is that while "we" have an obligation to protect each other's rights, we have a responsibility larger still—that of inventing an academic world consciously and explicitly adjusted to the huge variousness of the means by which men develop intellectual power and understanding. There are a hundred ways (mine are too crude and wordy: check) of building that assumption into a law-and-order document. And I'll sign and circulate, N., fight the good fight, the whole bit—I promise—once the assumption is built in.

But—apologies and thanks for the coffee—not until.

II

Meeting a Stranger

Journal of a Campus Strike

What do you do when it dawns on you that the life you chose, the career you prepared for, the work you love best, is sliding away, belongs more to memory or fantasy than to day-to-day reality? Well, whatever you do, you feel strange—by turns unbelieving, defensive, resentful . . . excited, overeager . . . frightened. For some in my profession—teachers who've been political men almost exclusively for close to a decade—the career and its savored intellectual labor disappeared long ago. Others had "the experience" in the moratoria and other class suspensions of 1969 and 1970. Some are still untouched, of course—they're facing the upcoming school year with confidence and relish not greatly changed from that of the past.

In my case "the experience"—in a non-violent, undramatic, innocuous version, to be sure—came at the end of twenty years of teaching (at Amherst College, in Massachusetts), at a time I was certain I'd found my way in my work. "Twenty years" has a portentous sound. It's not the years that count, it's that toward the end of the stretch I'd come on my own teaching style, something personal, not irresponsible, and capable—as though it were an independent source of energy, rather than a mere style—of generating questions fascinating (to me) in themselves. Simultaneously I'd learned how to link up my teaching self and my citizen self in satisfying ways—small tutorial projects in Mississippi, seminars with kindergarten and first-grade school teachers in Washington, D.C., lobbying for controlled shifts of curricular and admissions policies at my college. A way of saying it is that I knew where I was, believed I earned my pay, felt confident I'd improved immensely in the classroom over the years, felt pleased at my luck at capitalizing on chances to use teaching skills in settings less privileged than my home base: fulfillment looked near at hand.

Then came eruption: my interests, amusements, absorptions, evenings spent hunting what's most moving and easiest to miss in this or that play (texts to brood on with my Shakespeare seminar)—everything went off, ceased to occupy space in the mind or the feelings. It didn't matter what my subject was. It didn't matter that the *Lear* papers were tremendous or that I failed again with *The Merchant* or that *Antony* was still ahead, waiting to "redeem the term." It didn't matter that D. J. Enright's new little Shakespeare book was splendid—exhilarating not just because Enright is a capable critic but because time and time over (as it turned out) I'd conceived teaching problems exactly as he had done, and could therefore feel the lovely sense of a companionable, orderly world that wakes at any moment of "professional confirmation" . . . All of this was emptied out.

In theory spelling out what replaced it is needless: everybody knows the "campus strike story." But perhaps such stories have and always will have two centers, one that's over-reported, a congeries of declarations and resolutions, official actions, etc., and another that's at bottom shadowy and uncertain—an experience of displacement, of ceasing to possess a familiar and substantial world. Approaching the latter center means entering as a private person complete with envies, ambitions, etc., somebody groping about, adding events up on his own. The "story" is snippets, puzzles, bits of the past coming back, scratchings for motives, escalations of personal convictions into Necessary Policies, here and there a hard-bought glimpse of an honest-to-God factor, something sustainedly clear. One minute you think you have it and the next—

❋

Thousands and tens of thousands killed, the President and Cambodia on April 30, Kent State the day before yesterday, a week-long night of confusion, wrangling, fury, frustration . . . It calls for detachment, a wide view, and I haven't been delivering. Tonight George Kateb of Political Science—possibly our best mind— "galvanized the community." Because he behaved as he did, we're in the national movement, committed to the national strike. Speaking on the steps of Religion, a rally before faculty meeting, George introduced the "constitutional question," declared the White House had "overstepped itself," said flatly he sees a "constitutional crisis," and that for this reason academic protest is legitimate and necessary. —I was there, I was listening, but truthfully I didn't attend caringly to the argument. Distraction took me, I trivialized it.

We'd walked over to the campus together after supper, Benjy (my twelve-year-old) and I. Ben knew "Mr. Kateb" partly from the supper table, partly because George has lately been lecturing in the junior high school American government program. He also knows George as somebody with a solid record about the war—a strong vocal opponent for years—infinitely better than mine. I was evasive and when at length I woke up, my sons—even the older one at Columbia—showed tact and forbearance. They never mention my long "complicity," the hawkish frowns and grumblings. No taunts. Still, the sense of my fallibility has been overwhelming these last years, bad for my morale.

But I'm interrupting: Benj and I are waiting on the Chapin lawn in the May damp, and my head is busy (I may as well confess) thinking of lines of argument George might adopt that might not go down with my boy. It's conceivable, isn't it, that George will take this occasion to argue that even now nothing can justify the politicization of the campus. That would jibe with earlier statements of his. If George goes that way, I might step out ahead of him . . . "explain" his inflexibility to Benjy.

Why is there never enough time to explain things to children! Can I compete with George on his own ground? This is an exceptional man. You can sense it even in the Student Course *Critique*'s commentary. ("Professor Kateb includes the term 'political morality' in his description of both his courses. The student is consistently impressed with his commitment to a higher form of politics, his concern for the relationship between the art of politics and the 'pursuit of the good.' Professor K. is a man of strong opinions, but he is at his best when these opinions are challenged. . . . His exams are among the most educational at Amherst. . . . Grading is low. . . . It is very difficult to get a high grade. . . .") Last year during the class suspension George sat out under the trees in the quadrangle patiently dissecting the madness of institutional democratization, arguing (without taking any visible selfish joy in his position) that "excellence" could not survive anywhere save in a unified, single-standard, intellectual community. His talk to the Senior Assembly—very straightforward, no currying favor. ("One cannot lightly dismiss the authority of parents, the authority of elementary and secondary teachers; the authority of college teachers, and the general authority of superior experience and/or knowledge. . . . There is no quality more easily lost than scrupulousness when men act, especially when they think their cause good. They become impatient, and impatience can be productive of evil. . . . My fear is that the joys of participation . . . loosen attachment to procedures. . . . The company I want is the company I choose, and its numbers will be small. I hate the tribe. . . . There are many times when I want to be left alone, as I want to leave others alone. Live and let live; laissez-faire, laissez-passer. I beg you to make allowance for irreducible temperamental differences. . . .")

The audio is ready on the steps, Jefferson Airplane blaring forth "Volunteers of America." The lawns in front of the building have filled up—students, teachers, children, dogs. Ben and I in front. Noise, talk, dogs barking. There are scores of watchers on the dorm rooftops when George crosses the terrace, summoned to the microphone. A short, stocky, fortyish, Syrian bachelor, carefully dressed, black frill of hair, lively poetical eyes, crisp unrhetorical manner. "I don't know any answers," he begins. The quadrangle is instantly still, a thousand people intent. The side

of my face feels Benjy listening, eyes bright, lips apart. He's holding his knees. The world at attention. "I'm not sure I even know
the right questions to ask. I feel a deepened dismay and outrage.
I'm more upset by what has happened in the last few days than
about any of our government's policies over the last few years."
    George pauses, but doesn't look out toward his audience.
Impossible not to feel his worth and weight at this instant. He
speaks containedly, separating his sentences, separating himself
from his emotion. He believes, he says, that Presidents Kennedy,
Johnson and Nixon were alike in that they regarded political
life as "a test of manhood." Eisenhower did not suffer that burden.
But the point isn't to make comparisons, he says heavily. He
takes in his breath and begins again:

> My outrage and my dismay have deepened for a very simple and
> academic reason: Nixon's behavior in Cambodia indicates that
> the President of the United States now feels he can make any
> commitment he wants, largely because the people of this country
> are afraid that the alternatives to contradicting his will will be
> worse than backing it up. . . . Nixon has gone beyond the Con-
> stitution.

Given this situation, George goes on, there are no longer any
havens. He reminds us he's held to a vision of the academy as
"a haven for intellectual development," a place apart. (Benjy
doesn't frown at this.) As a teacher he's argued that "only on
extraordinary occasions should the academic community take a
stand." But now, he says, shaking his head, "I've overcome my
very deep scruples about seeing Amherst enter the public arena."
    That is all. Within an hour, the resolution cancelling classes
and initiating campus-wide political activity passes the faculty
meeting: "shutting it down to open it up." It's indeed been a
moment, an unusual turn: the voice of rebellion speaking through
the College's most effective critic of so-called "student rebellious-
ness." It deserves attention on its own terms, has meaning and
significance . . . And what if it didn't? What father wouldn't be
thankful that someone of George Kateb's quality figures im-
portantly in his son's imagination? Who wouldn't want a "significant elder" of this kind contending for space against Mick
Jagger or whomever?

—Benjy's standing up, applauding with the others. I watch him and feeling sinks in me. Cambodia, Nixon, Kent State, reserved rights—they aren't in my equation. No wide views, no seriousness. I'm merely "personal"—jealous, hurt. I envy George his place—it's as simple as that. I wish my son was on his feet for me.

❋

News, an unpredictable event: I've been appointed to the Steering Committee, the coalition organizing the Strike. I'm learning things: how a Scene begins to build in a college "disturbance," what it's like at the instant students believe at last they know what they want. Awake all night, they "man the phones" at "the information center" at "strike headquarters"—rooms in the basement of Religion. They're calling and being called, "writing," "doing research," "working with," "setting up," "checking that out," "putting it on the bulletin board . . ." "The hope is that the workshops *will not* be a one-day thing, but *will* evolve into Action Labs where people can continue meeting, discussing, *educating* and then *acting.*" "Power to the people" . . . —New Mexico is out, Connecticut is out, strike leaders meeting in San Jose, meeting in Washington, people in jail at Kent State, rumors, hundreds—well, find *out*, call Cleveland, call Akron,· call Miami U, got a friend in Ohio, Pittsburgh, West Virginia, call them all. . . . Faculty people are joining in. Dartmouth is talking computers, Princeton is on the Hill, Rochester's into "something tremendous." A 50-cent petition drive, 20 million signatures, $10 million for commercial spots—slick jobs. "Doyle Dane, a full-dress agency-planned anti-war saturation TV thing, maybe Jerry della Femina—you know, From those wonderful folks who brought you Pearl Harbor?" . . . In one day they've picked up $17,000! Beautiful. The *Times* ad is ready, a message from the Four Colleges, no, Five Colleges, a piece of a Sunday page impeaching Agnew for conspiring to cross state lines—violence, something, ten dollars a name. Sign here. My God look at the twenties in that hat!

My God, look at the calendar!

	10 AM	1 PM	8 PM
Mon	Vietnam	Cambodia	Indochina
Tue	Panthers	Political Repression	Repression
Wed	Corporate Power	Defense Establishment	Power Elite
Thur	Role of University	Selective Service	University
Fri	Domestic Politics	Political Protest	Political Action

Plus: 9 AM, draft counseling training—9:30, Information and Research Task Force—10, draft counseling—11, seminar on "canvassing techniques"—noon, draft counseling—1 PM, "pre-canvassing educational seminar (Implications of Foreign Policy for Domestic Issues)," organizational meeting for Wall Street March, rally at U Mass cage ("marshals and medics needed badly")—2 PM, women's lib—4, draft counseling—student assembly at 6, lectures after supper, dorm meetings at 11, midnight call for editorial workers on the job at Strike HQ. *Plus* workshops in every corner of the Valley: "Social Psychology of War," "Goals and Political Effectiveness of the Strike," "The Role of the Arts in Revolution (bring instruments)," "Biological Warfare," "Marx and Race," "Workers Socialist League," "Imperialism in the Mideast (Khalil Khalil, Halim Hussani)," "Palestinian Revolution," "Imperialism, Mil-Indus Complex," "General Rap on Strike," "Power of the Pres.," "Forms of Political Action," "Dissent and the Police," "Humanizing Each Other (under clump of trees at pond)," "Crowd Behavior and Crowd Violence," "School of Education as a Fascist Institution," "Observations of former member of Westmoreland Staff on Indochina War," "Hometown High School Involvement," "Fascism," "Self-survival in the Social Revolution," "Meditation and Politics," "Revolution of Love and Reason" . . .

Mimeo wars begin raging. (HELP! DRIVERS! MONEY! DESPERATE!) "Correspondence by all to Congress, state legislators and mass media . . . State coordinators needed" . . . "Green Carnival THIS WEEKEND. HELP NEEDED—work games (beanbags back in Agnew's mouth), work booths. ACT FAST! (Grace Church lawn ours)" . . . "Students knowing high-up corporation officers contact Joe Evans . . . contact Labor Unions" . . . "Canvassing in Holyoke 10 AM–2 PM–7 AM—*Canvassers and drivers desperately needed!*" . . . "RESEARCH AND INFORMATION NEEDS TYPISTS—meet in Converse Gold Room at 9:30 AM Friday." Marshals and medics for Washington Task

Force "REPORT TO ALL SOUL'S CHURCH. REMEMBER—
NON-VIOLENT!" Summer and Home Action Committee, Com-
mittee for a Continuing Presence in Washington, Committee to
Organize the High Schools, Committee to Organize the Prep
Schools, Afro–Am—

"Fantastic," say the experienced hands at the Steering Committee table. "Never seen anything like it." "The most fantastic
outpouring of interest—" "Incredible." The Chapel ceiling trem-
bles with applause at mass meetings—janitors wait outside in the
sun, afraid of overloaded balconies collapsing . . . Shouts, standing ovations, fists skyward, packed seminars, packed departmental student-faculty sessions . . . DON'T WASTE YOUR TIME
OR YOUR OPPORTUNITY—USE IT—WE NEED YOU. SEIZE
THE TIME!

—I remember when we were first married (granted, domesticity isn't relevant) and my father came to visit, he'd grin and
tell us we were kids, just "playing house." Something of this goes
through my head these mornings. We're playing, are we not?
We're children still? The question, What next? doesn't arise?
There's no tomorrow, this minute only is all that counts? . . .

✿

A three-hour panel discussion in the Chapel, finished at eleven.
I come off the platform with the others, pooped. A student asks
me to give a hand over at Chapin. Strike HQ. A lot of faculty
are helping. Students are up against it, finishing a booklet, sixty
pages, it's to help students when they try to get across their point
of view on issues to parents—when they go home. But the printer
has to have it tomorrow afternoon and if the thing's not finished
—The labor they've put into it—writing, etc. . . . . A waste. If I'd
do a section or two, any help at all . . . Dozens of girls and boys
and teachers scratching away, typing, proofing, on all three floors
of the building. I find a room and a machine, paper, the ms. . . .
Rubble everywhere. The Registrar's secretaries, girls in their
thirties, have been helping around the clock. Bleared eyes, beer
cups, butts, coffee, hands and foreheads with ink smears, mimeo
churning. The seminar table in a room I've taught in is the copy
desk, a dozen youngsters sitting around it, general editor in the

keyhole. Tom Wartenberg, the head man on the project, shuts the door behind us on a noisy hall, explains the drill calmly. He seems older to me, a full tone or two older, highly responsible. They have a typist freed for 2 AM so if I can possibly clean up the text by then . . . It's real bad—Repression, history of repression in America, showing we're not perfect, bad things happen, the impulse to gag the opposition runs deep . . . "Can I get you something? We're out of beer—"

I get at the job, thinking: not in twenty years of teaching have I refused a student an "extension." We live in a world without deadlines. Time hasn't got any nerves, it's flat and loose, "humane." Nobody insists. Nobody locally tightens the curb, the chin strap, makes the head sit smart. Get it done or else. It matters, somebody's *waiting* . . . An experience denied. Therefore we invent it for themselves. We want a taste of human urgency. And how generous we are! we'll even share the experience with others. . . . I grin at that—and at the mound of hard-selling SDS copy in my hand. I don't discount the war or the "constitutional issue" . . . But I believe part of the joy of this interruption lies in the quality of the experience, the impatience, the heightening of an evening, establishing a unit of time as something not to be sloped through, as something to be moved across nervously, toward an edge, a brink, a running out—! *Got* to get it done . . . Newell the printer can't handle it after 5 PM, he won't guarantee . . . he's not kidding. I feel *I* count too. Beautiful.

✿

A younger colleague in the Department came out of his door just now as I was heading for the water cooler. He had a folder, notes, books—*Anna Karenina*—in hand, obviously on his way to a class. Looked me straight in the eye. Yes, I'm teaching and I'm not even remotely ashamed of it. I'm proud of it. So said the look. Not pugnacity but pride and resolution. Heightened sense of personal probity. If when all about you lose their heads . . . The faculty resolutions specify thus far that those who wish to go on teaching may do so, no coercion. That won't change. But here's a side effect of "non-coercion." Teacher and taught feel themselves in a condition of "despiteness." Despite obstacles, despite majority dementia, say the hardrocks *and* the honest conservatives, *we* persevere. Humor or playfulness, imaginative ease —can they survive that sense of intransigent dutifulness? the feeling of embattled beleaguered virtue? the feeling that the man on strike across the hall—once a colleague—is now a kind of Enemy? I think there's no such thing, when most of us quit, as an uncoercive atmosphere. I ask Jack what he's teaching, we have a stilted conversation about Dolly with her kids in the bathhouse, and about Anna's talk about birth control—can "they" get the moral tone of that? I am trying to show him that the world of letters is still real to me, nothing matters more. He's showing me he doesn't hold this "situation" personally against me . . . What embarrassments! A moment like this shows you the beauty of college life on non-emergent occasions. How wearing it is, upholding your character!

*

The worst problem, I begin to see, is "placing" yourself. I felt it strongly this afternoon listening to Henry Commager and Leo Marx in the Chapel. They're far and away our most potent speakers "from the left." They have detractors, yes, but again and again at the disasters—the murder of Dr. King, face-offs with the Marine recruiters—they've been the men who have found words for the rest of us, named the community's concern, rage, resolution. They were working hard just now, attempting to inspire the student body as a whole to unprecedented political effort. "What is the Academy to do," Henry asked, "—and remember the Academy is seven million strong?" His answer was that we must fling ourselves forward in a "crusade":

> Let us turn in this crusade of rescue and restoration, turn back to the spirit of the men who animated the Republic, who wrote the Constitution and the Bill of Rights into the Constitution, who established the principle of the superiority of the civil over the military authority, who rejected all secrecy in government, who put their confidence in and their bets on enlightenment, on education as a great panacea which would enable this people and this nation to achieve progress and happiness.

Let us be animated not just by their example but by the admonitions addressed to us, addressed indeed to all people in the greatest of all orations, that of Pericles to the people of Athens. As I quote from him let us draw strength, "For the busy spectrum of our great city's life as we have it before us day by day, falling in love with her as we see her, remember that all this greatness she owes to men: the fighter's daring, the wise man's understanding of his duty, and the good man's self-discipline in its performance." And he added what may be the greatest phrase in literature: "Knowing that the secret of happiness is freedom and the secret of freedom a brave heart, do not idly stand aside at the onset of the enemy."

I pulled back from this, partly in stock response to Ciceronianism, partly in a flicker of irrepressible risibility—the gap between the ancient heroic mode and the characteristic costume and posture of the lads spread out in the aisles with their dogs. And then a minute later—it's as though all I am is fastidiousness— I was pulling back from Leo's oratory. Leo was arguing in a plainer style that the students must *believe* in the strike, hold high their faith in its meaning and potential. You'll hear people wondering, he said, whether

> the strike and the related activties [may] not accentuate the animosity between the students and the universities on the one hand, and the people of the United States on the other? Isn't this militancy dangerous? Won't it produce a counterreaction in excess of the action? How can a strike of students influence the Great Silent Majority who already knows what they believe and doesn't like them? How can we go out in the street and talk to the people who are so prejudiced against us?

But they must control their doubts. They must see the Strike in its true scale:

> I say this is the most comprehensive action of colleges and universities in our history . . . For the first time in my memory the faculty and the students and the administration are together . . . seven million people are potentially here speaking to the American people from an institution which is vital to the way of life as we have known it, and that we are saying something to the American people . . . This strike is a signal that the present policies of the American government, if persisted in, will eventually destroy the structure of higher education in America, and that we have brought the universities and colleges in this country to a halt. And that's the important fact, because it threatens to

bring them to a halt permanently. . . . The reason it threatens
to bring them to a halt permanently is not that we have a plan
to bring them to a halt, but because there is a fundamental and
underlying incompatability between a society devoted to war and
racism and imperialism and the principles of higher education for
which we all stand . . . This strike is inherently a political act of
immense consequences and potentiality.

I pulled back from this because queasy about extravagant expectations. But it's painful being with those who're simply looking for provocation to pull back. Some students know precisely
how to "take" these voices—Henry's and Leo's. About Henry's
grand old rhetoric—does it really harm them to hear how men
once sounded the alarm bell to each other?—some students would
say: Mr. Commager's an older man, he's seventy or something,
he loves England, knows all the orators, that's the way he *wants*
people to talk in moments of trouble, so it's appropriate. And
about Leo's "immense consequences," some think: Mr. Marx cares
deeply, he hates the smugness, the complacency, and this hatred
forces him into exaggeration . . . Take his voice for what it is:
absolutely sincere. Repeat: I think many students thought these
thoughts. But I'm not positive and I ought to record I was uncomfortable.

*

More on Commager-Marx: when they got into their "dispute,"
it was genuinely uncomfortable. The argument was about the
best kinds of political action under the circumstances. Henry was
scathing about demonstrations ("nothing more irrelevant than
demonstrations . . . a misuse of your power, your authority, your
time, your thought"). He told the students, "however you may
feel about the system we now have, what you want—I am confident—is results—that's what we all want—and we must ask ourselves how we get results." The answer is conventional political
activity directed at changing the composition of the Congress:

Ours is still a political system subject to change and subject to
control by political mechanisms . . . Politics can be effective.
Politics can change the Congress this fall and Congress and the
Presidency two years from now. And as far as I can see this is
the only way in which we can get change, the only way in which

we may hope to rescue ourselves from the follies and the wickedness in which we are now engaged. Politics can strengthen the hands of those who may put an end to the madness of Cambodia and Vietnam and may force what is more important in the long run—a reconsideration of the Cold War, for it is in that framework of the Cold War that we conduct our war in Southeast Asia . . . These things can be controlled only by the political mechanisms . . . I call upon you to rally to the political arena as you rallied to the political arena in 1968 with such spectacular results.

Leo said no:

. . . there's one glaring omission in what [Professor Commager] said. He appeals to you to enter the political arena and as I understood him he defines the political arena as efforts in the American electoral system to elect peace candidates or favorable candidates next November . . . I think that he ignores one simple fact: You have already entered the political arena. You're there. You're part of the largest, most comprehensive and militant act by American students and faculty in the history of this Republic. And we seem in the discussions of the last two days to lose sight of this—that we're in politics, that this [Strike] is a profound political act.

He went on to claim the reason the strike mattered in political terms wasn't that it was going to alter general public opinion throughout the country. The aim was to scare the country's elites, make them worry about total national chaos:

We tend to ignore the inherent efficacy of the strike not on public opinion directly but on those elites which control and influence the policies of this country. The sons and daughters of the professional and the governmental and the business and the educational elites—all those people in this country who have great influence and who want their sons and daughters and their grandchildren to go on getting the kind of higher education which we represent . . . The decision-making institutions of this society interlock, and when the President of Amherst College sits over there in his office and answers the 'phone calls from the alumni and the trustees, and they say, "What are you doing, why are you letting those students push you around," he has to say, "Look, the faculty is with the students and the administration is with the students, and the only alternative is to see the place burn down, so we better be with the students, because we're all threatened." And I think this idea is beginning to get across. The elites which are locked into this system are connected to us, and they don't see how their way of life in this country can continue if the universities fall.

As I say, I wasn't unsympathetic. If Henry came for a drink tonight, I'd ask whether it isn't possible that the roots of the Strike lie in campus disaffection—not alone in Cambodia. The idea of the College as Athens or some other perfect place, the idea that the nagging problems are all out there—items for Capitol Hill, Congressional action, etc.—I don't think it'll wash. And as for Leo and talk about getting to the elites. Suppose you truly believe that the social enclaveism of our College—the social and moral climate engendered by it—is at best an ambiguous value, if a value at all: how can you turn around so enthusiastically to the exploitation of elitist "advantages"? And then beyond that: is it right ever to excite the young with strong imaginings of themselves as terrorizers? Those bits about burning the place down—what's the good of it? I know Leo told himself that they, the students, must somehow be given a feeling that what they're doing can have consequences, isn't empty . . . And he's right about that. And he's face to face with the problem of how to do this without helping them to imagine the consequences—a nervous telephone call by the President of the College, an imagined conversation, some auditory images of "impact." But still—

The meeting ended wildly. I was in the middle of casuistical exercises, intricacies, undecided about getting up and sounding like the voice from the right, when in comes the storm. LeRoy Howes roars up from below, grabs the mike, damns the "white devil liberals—" He was fierce. Again I have the stock response. I thought, Sit down, LeRoy, it's an impropriety, breach of decorum, order is necessary, each speaks in his turn, personal abuse unthinkable. But I'll also admit that I knew at least one side of what he meant, and I thought—on that side—he had a point.

*

"Placing yourself"—I said that was the problem, but no, I'm wrong. The problem is seeing the relatedness of behavior. The Configuration. Seeing how it all links up, making moral judgments a mess. This afternoon I understood that Leo was forced to "invent" an impact for this Interruption because none can be seen by the students or the rest of us. So he has to take the step, he has to say a mildly inflammatory word. But here's the crux: if there had been some openness in the equation, he wouldn't have felt that obligation. And there isn't any: there's only canniness, sound administrative cool. Why is it, after all, that "no impact" can be detected? Because the President of the College, Calvin Plimpton, is determined not to let any be detected. He's determined, that is, to allow no one to put him in the position of being the Enemy of the Strike. A day or two ago he read aloud, to an assembly of radical student leaders and "concerned" faculty, a letter he was sending to Amherst alumni. The letter states that "I am deeply sympathetic with the present sweep of anti-war sentiment . . . I have strong misgivings about the wisdom of the Cambodian decision and the techniques of the Nixon Administration in dealing with student dissent." These sentences had an impact on us. They connected themselves with a telegram the President announced he (and other Presidents) had sent to Nixon immediately after the first Cambodia speech—"implore you to consider the incalculable dangers of an unprecedented alienation of America's youth," etc. The effect was to suggest that the "comprehensiveness" Leo talked about was really genuine—the Administration was indeed "one of us," determined to bend its full weight to these oars.

But tonight I read the mail and there's a copy of this "same" letter to the alumni, and it turns out that the document the President read aloud at the public meeting ("We're sending this letter") was, as the phrase goes, "only a draft." The letter actually mailed began with a joke about students (they "feel that they are the ones who have discovered poverty, injustice and racism"), contained no word of critique of White House policy, no "deep sympathy"—no "sweep of sentiment," etc. Am I getting this clear? I know I'm tired. The point is the President read one letter and sent another. And the point is that Leo and some others who doubted the Administration's solidarity, who were sure that behind the equable, agreeable, unflappable exterior there had to be deep reservations and a stubborn opposition— well, we're right. There's no openness anywhere.

Yes, these are complicated matters. A competent President

never needlessly provides a target in his own person for rage seething on his campus. He knows it's foolish to allow his disapproval of protest leaders to appear in general view. Never Incite, Never Exacerbate. He tries to combine a high level of personal visibility with a low profile of authority. He maintains a seemly eagerness for interchange, dialogue, negotiation. He resists as long as possible and then a while longer every temptation to a show of force. He waits patiently—let it run its course, let them talk themselves out, end of term will come, enough rope, etc. But much that Cal Plimpton has done so far (last year the same) fits only very roughly within these rubrics.

I'm not charging Chicanery. Even at the worst, the list of deeds wouldn't look impressive—mere Realpolitik. The very success of these presidential measures edges us back—so far—from catastrophic crises where you call the police or order them out and thereafter bring on loud debates—while heads are beaten—about rashness, courage, shrewdness or whatever. But no matter how undramatic they are, the things the President has done are having an effect. He hasn't merely "maintained a low profile." He's unsympathetic with the strike but he's already twice made himself out to be a kind of leader of protest, stopping militants from drawing clear lines between themselves and him. He did this last spring, too, during the Moratorium—another suspension of classes. And now there's this new evidence—begging to be "exploited" . . . One view of the crisis to one constituency and another to the next, messages rewritten after having been presented as finished facts, moves in any direction that'll postpone "confrontation." When you have all this in mind, as I say, it's easy to sympathize with Leo's frustration, his need to demonstrate that the trenches over there aren't empty, this isn't a war of shadows, etc.

—And therefore why not whip up a storm? Why not a direct charge of duplicity aimed at the President? One reason is that nobody's got the will for it, not the faculty or the student body. And the reason for this, in turn (so I think), is that people sense Cal Plimpton is in a trap too. . . . He behaves as he does, not because he's the Trustees' man on campus, not because duplicity comes easy, not because he's thought out a series of Machiavellian moves. He does what he does (the analysis may be sentimental, that's true) because *he doesn't know how to draw a line.*

Why so? I can't answer without pretending to know from inside a style of life that I don't know. What is more pretentious than somebody not born to an Upper Establishment life dogmatizing about the boredom within that life, the desirability of escaping? Still it's a fact (I think) that people who escape the life often speak of it as tiresome—same people, attitudes, round of pleasures, feeling of marginality or functionlessness. Despite radical chic, the flexible Social Register, incursions of minorities, there's a stiffness in "life at the top." "They" know the action lies elsewhere. If you want an "interesting life"—Rockefeller-style, Kennedy-style, Harriman-style, Plimpton-style—you necessarily move into competition for power and authority with self-made men—figures on the way up, people "right off the streets." All the advantages are yours, yes—but still, some who try fail. Some who succeed see it as salvation—they're honestly grateful for their release from boredom and frivolity. And—here's the point of all this—maybe it's shaky—the escapees pay for their release by adopting a special sort of mod noblesse oblige (what's special about it?) aimed at banishing "differences."

The rules of the game are self-made, naturally. And you can't turn yourself into an insider merely by obeying them. The man of privilege remains a kind of exotic. Calvin Plimpton, M.D. and President, is a meditative physician among college presidents. He was previously a student of Zen among the internists at the College of Physicians and Surgeons. He was a "Chaucerian" in the Riverdale where quarter million dollar houses and Northeast Harbor summers are standard form. Now he's a quasi-Beautiful Person among a passel of profs. (I am being unsympathetic, true.) But even though he's a step "outside," he at least can work, and not at exotica; he can teach internal medicine or set professors' wages or otherwise function in a substantial serious world. And he can do it without guilt, because he heeds the rules laid down by his kind for his kind. By this I mean that he behaves always as though differences among men are much exaggerated. He turns away unnoticingly, whenever possible, from intransigent characters who try to set themselves off from others. And he evades—jokes and humor are the ticket here—he evades all reminders from others of the efforts of some of his kind to avoid contact with the mob.

And this is the trap: the instinct or obligation to amusingly minimize differences. (It doesn't make a Satan. It does make a man sometimes artfully unskilled at argument, hesitant about justifying his case, bored with the job of clarifying issues.) The President's instincts often lead him toward comedy. He's continually discovering that this or that allegedly unassimilable individual or reputation is in fact a clubbable man—Great Fun. Home from a *Paris Review* anniversary party, he smiles across his desk at you as a meeting starts—smiles across and says he's just seen this little Mr. Mailer and he doesn't see what the fuss is about. "A perfectly nice fat little fellow, nice as he could be. Great fun." Implicit is a suggestion that it's by accident all present missed Mr. Mailer—no reason for all present not to have been there, beautiful people, Mr. Mailer, the Plimptons, the Committee are at one, no differences obtain, Great Fun. The same sort of suggestion surfaces during a debate about the Trustee decision to vote its proxies with management during the Campaign GM fight, and to advise the faculty please to tend its business. Ted Greene in History rises to argue that the proposed addition of public members to the GM board is hardly a blow to management. The people suggested for the jobs include unviolent men like John Rockefeller of West Virginia, who, says Ted, is married to the daughter of yet another unfrightening person, Senator Percy. What's more, he assumes the President knows these people well and trusts them, otherwise why would he serve with them— as he presently does—on the Exeter board of trustees? The President looks momentarily sheepish, then his charming face collapses in mock tears and weeping. "She's gone, Sharon's gone," he cries in a heartstruck falsetto . . . We're briefly puzzled, and then it dawns—of course, "Sharon" would be Sharon Percy, yes yes, a beautiful young girl, yes yes, the President is talking again, being explicit now—John Rockefeller's gone off the Exeter board, completed his service, and therefore: "Sharon's" gone, weep for her passing. The quality of the comic turn depends on our knowing how it goes with the gorgeous and the great: all members know, love, share "Sharon," feel bereft, have had great fun.

And the truth is that the train goes both ways. This interchangeability of position and place—erosion of human difference by sleight of manner—moves in every direction, not just up. Our President lives in an Empsonian symmetrical pastoral where all shepherds are comfortably lords and all lords shepherds. We're more often invited to stand with him as clubman or trustee than as humble worker, cop, janitor or super, but those jobs are open —on occasion he takes them up. I remember the early days of undergraduate sexual liberation, parietal rules just banished, and the maids and campus cops and janitors outraged by the evidences of promiscuity spread out in the dorms. The President "saw from below," saw with the janitors, sympathetically, on that occasion, and assumed we'd do the same.

And just a month ago, come to think, he stood with the hard hats, sharing with the huge forgotten majority the new keenness for breaking skulls. This was a breathtaking bit. I suppose it's behind the coldness I feel. Hard to believe that the hard hat sensibility breathed around here—this rich, delicately placed, lush river valley plateau. No city, no crowd, no violence in the papers . . . Loveliness beyond smutching. Elsewhere there's "trouble," wanton defacing of property . . . "One" reads of it in the papers. But "that kind of thing doesn't happen here." We've got "a different class of student," we "give no provocation to violence," we abolished ROTC in the fifties, we provide "our blacks" with our best-known and most interesting building, architecturally speaking, as a Culture Center. We're immune. —But the immunity ends. Somebody trashes the War Memorial—a superb quarter of the campus, a sundial circle laid into a hillside opening to the south—a view of the whole green valley, playing fields, bird sanctuaries, forest preserves, uninterrupted by houses for miles on toward the Holyoke Range. All my feeling for this College rises here. Stone benches, a raised dial carved with the names of sons of the College killed in the first two world wars of this century . . . a Western expanse, marvelous tranquility.

It was trashed in the spring, desecrated with obscenities and the peace symbol. The President is asked to comment at faculty meeting. He speaks seriously. He's just come, he says, from the Buildings and Grounds retirement party, Wes Jensen and three or four others who've given their lives to the College and were retiring, and it was all those fellows could talk about, and they were saying if they ever saw anybody doing that, well, the President says, several of them, they said, We'd go after them with baseball bats, we'd just club their heads off like rabbits. Cal's manner dissociates neither himself nor his listeners from the enthusiastic clubbing, sets up no distance between his views and those of the short, squat, bullnecked electrician whose close-cropped gray head is all hard-bunched force, a man who travels the campus with a boxer dog and could easily play Lee Cobb playing a state trooper behind black leather, glaring wraparound shades. Beat them with baseball bats.

—But I'm not getting it. . . . Anecdote doesn't do the work, it comes out snide no matter how it's meant. The "relevant truth of character" lies not in particular deeds in particular situations, but in a coherent style—a self-consistent way of perceiving events and circumstances, an unvarying mode of speech. Calvin Plimpton's habitual pliancy, his compulsion to erase or minimize differences, shows up at every faculty meeting. My God, argument has to fight for the right to breathe! The parliamentarian is encouraged to rest easy about laxities of procedure, over-permissive, good-hearted, over-jocular referrals of moot points. . . . Lately we've thrown out the custom of accepting presidential calls on voice votes and the other night the whole house heard the President say to the Dean, after counting hands on his side of the room, that the yeas on some issue were "about thirty." "About!" came an incredulous cry. "About?" People turned to each other, half-laughing, half-speechless in unbelief—damn the quarrel-mongers, damn the Roundheads . . .

It's an habitual mode, that's the key. The President invariably speaks as though the task of putting others less well-placed in life than himself in situations open to him couldn't conceivably be a problem. The visiting candidate for a medical school deanship will have to be gotten round to Club A or Club B, he's bound to like it. The interested student of Middle East problems will have to be "gotten out to Beirut" first thing—or into the Foreign Policy Association—or down to the Tavern or wherever. No obstacle . . . In his conversation he regularly imagines the person talking to him—no matter how junior in years or position—as occupying a position above him, as saying briskly to him, "Well now, Plimpton, old fruit, you're dead wrong . . ." His smiling, lazily uttered slogans, much-chuckled-at ("Well now, Harold, we don't want to think about that, we just want to worry about moving the ball down the field"), are heavy with disbelief in the necessity of division. His apparent confidence that difference really has been abolished makes him take risks in public situations that most people in his job—scared of the standard sometimes invoked in judgments of the high-placed—would never take.

No, I'm not claiming the President himself is deceived by his own gestures—that's naïve. I'm saying he's trapped by a habit, a tic belonging to a class—the privileged who can't be blamed for wanting to distract the eye from privilege and who do so by seeing all the world as one. I'm saying we have a President who won't be flushed out, can't be baited, won't argue. I'm saying this leads teachers and students to try to sting—because if you haven't got an opposition on the scene, then how can you sustain a sense of focused grievance? And I'm saying that the net effect of this unflushable quality is to sustain a world precisely as the Establishment wants it to be sustained. The thirteenth President of Amherst, like many who preceded him, came to his post charged with the job of maintenance. The age was crazy for change. The determination of the managers is that change shall be resisted to the point at which resistance compromises the institutional future. It's understood that accommodation to pressure will under certain circumstances be unavoidable. But accommodation shouldn't overgo necessity except as a calculated gamble, as a strategy for postponing graver changes than those momentarily urged.

Well and good: the President has been in office for eleven years. In that period many institutions comparable to this have undergone campus violence or major changes in modes of governance ("opening up"). We've "endured" neither. No student votes in faculty meeting. No student sits in faculty meeting. No faculty member or student sits or votes at meetings of trustees. No student has an effective voice in hiring or tenure decisions. No student has an effective voice in the choice of candidates for honorary degrees (faculty opinion has lately been consulted but as yet to virtually no consequence). No change in admissions policy has occurred in the past decade. The fraternity system, its abolition recommended by full faculty vote, survives unaltered, heavily subsidized by Trustee appropriations. The endowment of the College has substantially increased. A major building program has been successfully completed. Student agitation for new forms of governance has failed to issue in an effective student assembly and no student-faculty alliance exists. Machinery for selecting student members of curricular committees has broken down and there is—or was before the Strike began—serious doubt that the student newspaper (a dependable voice of disaffection) will publish next year. All we have—and we've had it for exactly what? eight days?—is this Strike.

And yet and yet and yet: the College remains, according to the figures, with the exception of Radcliffe, the most over-applied undergraduate institution in America. The resistance to change, in sum, has been successful.

But no, that's the wrong direction. I'm not talking about success or failure of the resistance. The subject is the *unwilled character* of the resistance. I am saying that, just as Leo Marx is "victimized," unfree, so too is the President: his "policy" is far less schematic, programmatic, Machiavellian, even at its most apparently duplicitous, than we want to believe. Here, too, the ineluctable personal dimensions demand to be "figured in." You have to consider a man's past, his family style, the bearing of class issues . . . "When you haven't the devil to fight, it's just that much worse."

Still: there is an enemy. I feel this more strongly than before. Proper names are lacking, but the obligation to struggle is not. *Contend.*

*

Note on habit: regardless of interruption, the mind continues pumping. Or it tries to, incapable of breaking every habit at once. That clump of words just set down about the President of the College, the relation between class position and academic policies, etc.: the "analysis" flowed out as though ruminating about presidents and presidencies was a regular occupation. It's not: I've probably thought a dozen times more about our President today than in all the years of his reign . . . What can you do? If you're used to thinking, if circumstances stop you from fiddling with books, you're bound to think about something, always—even if to small purpose.

❋

An aside on "class matters." The President spends himself on the abolition of the sense of difference. I work—this dawns on me just now, at least in this particular way—I work in exactly the opposite direction. For days now I've started an argument whenever a workshop or a speaker claims "we" can be of incalculable influence on community opinion by "going to the people." My line is that believing in the readiness of others to hear "us" in these special days implies ignorance of the consequences of separateness and enclaveism in ordinary times. My purpose is to propose the relevant question—I don't care how tired it is or I am: it has to come up—about right relations between college and society.

Today's occasions of "controversy" were varied. I talked at the morning mass meeting, invoking Mill and Sartre, trying to demonstrate that people who go forth from one self-contained enclave, assuming their words and meanings can be taken with them, assuming their "correct" understandings will be quickly fathomed by others, are victims of a bad education—an education you can't improve except by modifying the enclaveism. ("'A man must be able to hear opinions [different from his own],' said Mill, 'from persons who actually believe them, who defend them in earnest, and do their very utmost for them. He must know them in their most plausible and persuasive form; he must feel the whole force of the difficulty which the true view of the subject has to encounter and dispose of . . .' What in the college life as led here helps us to comprehend that 'whole force'?") In the afternoon a psychologist, an English teacher with experience in ghetto projects, and I ran a session about notions and feelings concerning the student and the professor likely to turn up among Valley truck farmers, small town merchants, ghetto parents. Tonight, a disaster, I took out after the honored guest—Johnson's Labor Secretary, Willard Wirtz, a College trustee—for creating extravagant hopes of instant influence among the students (they were cheering his slambang rousing speeches), and for failing to concede that the kinds of overnight social transformation he had them dreaming on could never be achieved *de haut en bas*. And, oh yes, lunchtime in the dining hall. I was again, in a session with a group of students, arguing self-righteously about those who incite young people of privilege to believe in the sameness of men. Aren't they sentimentalizing confrontation, oversimplifying social process, replacing "modest, slow, molecular, definitive, social work" with magic? My text was a poem circulating on the campus—Richard Wilbur had sent it north from Wesleyan as encouragement to canvassers:

TO THE STRIKERS

Go talk to those who are rumored to be unlike you,
And whom, it is said, you are so unlike.
Stand on the stoops of their houses and tell them why
You are out on strike.

It is not yet time for the rock, the bullet, the blunt
Slogan which fuddles the mind toward force.
Let the new sound in our streets be the patient sound
Of your discourse.

Doors will be shut in your faces, I do not doubt.
Yet here and there, I think, there may start,
Much as the lights blink on in a block at evening,
Changes of heart.

They are your houses; the people are not unlike you.
Talk with them, then, and let it be done
Even for the grey wife of your nightmare sheriff
And the guardsman's son.

I wasn't at my best—too much easy "making-fun-of." I talked against the poem's account of how a movement of mind occurs, how a man takes a step toward comprehension of another man's views:

                    . . . there may start,
Much as the lights blink on in a block at evening,
Changes of heart.

No no no—all petulance, I was. The ruling assumption that the "others" are there to be educated, talked with, jollied up at the convenience of "our" nobly self-sacrificing selves—that's Ivy con-descension. Men live without sympathy, for years they're pressed to contain themselves, narrow the band of speech, desire, interest, experience. And then at the moment of crisis—Pow! All Hail Breakout, no limits. Some crank may shut your pious face out, tell you to arse off, Sonny—but the others (bless them) are wait-ing, waiting for the College Man to come and explain what's what.

Student (interrupting, defensive):	But, sir, Wilbur knows that. He was just trying to help. He wanted to do something —be encouraging . . . What can a person do if he's a poet? . . .
Professor (acerb, scoffing):	He can inform himself. Poe-try should be at least as well-informed as prose . . .

I don't like myself at this—or I like myself too much. But I can't let it alone. Always when these moments of interruption come I can't shake off the longing to say My Thing, my only "relevant" thing. We don't know what it's like elsewhere, our truth exists wholly in an enclosed world. Even Lear and Cordelia mean something else off campus. And for all the self-inflation and possible opportunism in carrying the message, I don't con-ceed it's insincere. I remember the "Negro colleges" last month on my southern trip—Virginia State at Petersburg, Alabama A & M, a couple more. They're like stripped government build-ings—no "beautiful objects," no rug on the President's floor, no pictures, not a hint of the terms of a furnished life, a soft-edged world. The idea of expressing yourself or a relation to the past in the shape and color of a room—it's not there. Mary Holmes Junior College in West Point, Mississippi, all over again. —So the Society of Fellows at Eliot House should send a few of those Turkey carpets piled on each other in the Common Room? —No, the job is to hold in mind, as you imagine going forth "with the word," that the place you go to cannot imagine the ideas of har-mony and softened ease that are the contours of your thought, that lay out the inner landscape . . . they have another beat. The

Ivy university is, by inheritance, an aristocratic world: the "game" of interchangeability suits it, the life of the lord is its life through and through . . . a "classless" unified world. Where else on earth could anybody *read* Jonson on "Penshurst"?

—I can feel the shakiness of my "understandings"—the President no doubt feels the shakiness of his. So what should I say: We Need Both?

*

Participation explosion note: today's mail brings three letters from the college—Franklin and Marshall—where I'm to give a Commencement talk in a week or two. One student, two teachers. They're being helpful, offering advice about the speech and actually it *is* helpful, though (naturally) none of the three agrees with the others. Factions everywhere.

*

This morning I was sitting in the snack bar with a friend— just after the Steering Committee—when David Eisenhower came in alone. Except possibly for three blacks at "their" table, hardly a man of the maybe thirty in the room—this is how it felt—hardly one of us missed the entrance, was unconscious of this famous contemporary choosing silver, tray . . . hardly a man not watching through shoulders or ears. Yet no glance went toward him. The idea communicated was unconcern absolute. No "satisfaction" offered, no lessening of self by confessions of interest in a White House son-in-law at an hour of tension. David ate alone, left alone: and the look of unself-preoccupation, of comfort, of non-disturbance, of good nature, didn't leave his face. Seeking no eye, he didn't evade any either—"no satisfaction offered," no defiance offered. I felt the egalitarianism of the elite and the cruelty of children at the same time. A fair contest maybe—but still anyone would have wanted it otherwise. The children of the lucky middle class—the liberally educated, the uncelebrated but healthy and competent offspring of the beef-and-bullshot executive and professional classes—these have their pride too, and between them and David Eisenhower no steps lead up or down: a complete democratization of relationships. He's no more than we are, why give him the time of the day?

Of course even this isn't so simple. David's been a "very special kind of circumstance." People see him—some people—as an embodiment of the conflict betwen political or hierarchical principles and those of ordinary morality. Twice in his time here David has spoken in outright provocation. And because of the power of the name and place to "bring it all back home"—to incarnate the gap between authority and everybody else—both gestures were noticed. The first came last year during the moratorium. The "moratorium community" passed resolutions calling for a new charter of college government, new admissions policies, new wage scales for non-academic employees, coeducation . . . At the height of the episode, Leo Marx roused a mid-morning crowd with a proposal that "the College" write a letter to President Nixon telling him about student unrest, and warning him against underestimating the depth of feeling. Later Leo, the Dean and others drafted a letter that was mailed over the signature of the President of the College. ("Dear Mr. President . . . We believe that we must speak out to make clear that much of the turmoil among young people and among those who are dedicated to humane and reasoned changes will continue. It will continue until you and the other political leaders of our country address more effectively, massively, and persistently the major social and foreign problems of our society. Part of this turmoil in universities derives from the distance separating the American dream from the American reality . . .")

The response from the White House, written by Presidential Assistant Moynihan, was slow coming, but the response elsewhere was swift. The *Times* put the College on the front page and then a few days later came a lead editorial acclaiming the "Amherst Declaration." (. . . "it is clear that great numbers of idealistic and normally moderate students fail to oppose the radical forays, not because they approve of lawlessness, but because they are sincerely troubled and severely frustrated by much of what they— as well as many of their elders—know to have gone wrong with their colleges and their country. It is for them that President Calvin H. Plimpton of Amherst College appealed to President Nixon.")

Other Eastern places "ratified" the "Declaration" in their own faculty meetings. The *New Republic* and other magazines editorialized enthusiastically about the "Declaration." The College was news, and young Eisenhower, in the capital for a weekend, was asked about it by the wire services. Did he know about the letter? What'd he think, how had it come to pass, etc.?

David was harsh, rapping the "coercive" campus left. The "Amherst Declaration" couldn't represent the feelings of its alleged author—the President of the College, he said, had signed it "at the point of a gun." In short, liberals were bullies and tyrannizers, the college leader had to sell out to them, the much-vaunted "morality of the moratorium" was a straight-out political power grab. David's "enemies," their sense of personal purity perhaps momentarily heightened by the "moratorium experience," were infuriated by this version of events, this refusal to "rise above the level of partisanship." —And the same alleged Eisenhowerian stubbornness reappeared, just a couple of weeks ago, when David again stirred up the media with remarks "against the College." He let fall to the papers that he thought the doings of the student commencement committee were a slight to his family. (Several Eisenhowers were planning to come to commencement— "the family is big on graduations"; the student commencement committee had proposed I. F. Stone of I. F. Stone's *Newsletter*, or Cesar Chavez, leader of the striking grapepickers, as commencement speaker; young Eisenhower considered that either might stimulate demonstrations that would be "embarrassing" to his grandmother.) This second prod produced instant counter-protest. The student paper editorialized directly against him by name. It returned to the gunpoint remark, said it "demeaned the spirit of concern which the Plimpton letter imparted," and demonstrated that Eisenhower was "careless in his regard for his fellow students and inept in his dealings with the national press." It went on to assess the consequences of Eisenhower's comments about commencement—a cutoff of further contributions by alumni among them—and declared: "Eisenhower was insulting. Insulting to his classmates, to Mr. [I. F.] Stone, and to Amherst College . . ."

It's hard to think of young David as "insulting"—the cheerful, resilient, boyish, impulsive quality of the features and gestures smooth the cut of the adult political goad. I remember he once elected a course I taught—over-enrolled that year—and after the first class somebody asked what he was like—I was puzzled. I'd missed the name on the class lists—150 students—and had barely glanced at the crowd on opening day, depressed about paper-grading ahead. I resolved to rubberneck next time, and the experience was curious. As I walked through the door to the second class, two days later, an as yet unalphabeticized room, I knew just where to look. His face or grin had fastened itself at the place he occupied two days before—or else the vivacity and health of countenance (it truly is enormous) stamped its location on the Unconscious. Anyway, I knew where to look, and there young David materialized, meeting my glance with full expectation, also with the great life-relishing grin that puts straight before you not just Billy Budd (as Norman Mailer once wrote) but the grandfather at his best—to me a fine sight. —Hard to believe in him as "insulting."

But the point of interest and sadness was the readiness to cry Insult. I grant you David Eisenhower's happy self-assurance isn't at every moment winning. But is his an easy life? Would it be so for my sons? The very famous, young and old, have to cultivate—in order to keep off those unsure of the difference between good manners and bids to intimacy—an inhibition of deference. Looked at from outside the thing resembles self-love. And that inhibition spoils innocence—the nice openness, guilelessness, belief in the world's goodness that perfect a young man's beauty. You fall back on a self-regarding question (How much time will they want, how much do I have to give?) and it steals away the charm of the flower that is what it is, and you're left with aware-ness of your symbolic dimensions. Together with the puppy-dog likability and the neighbor kid in David Eisenhower, there was a touch of awareness of one's symbolic dimension, and on occasion he played from it as a strength.

And was played back to in kind, not from below: that needs repeating. No matter what else was implicit in these social con-tests, off on the margins of Political Dispute, they did tell the truth about the enclave. Somebody might suppose that young Eisenhower's attendance at our unimposing College would have confirmed for our obscurer selves the chosen-ness of our place, its national prominence, our own good luck. Wasn't David often "with the President of the United States"? Might it not be from David's reports that the summit of government learned what it knew of schools and scholars generally? Weren't the classmates subtly dignified, was not College life heightened, because of the placement of this young man of fame?

Thanks no. We have pretensions of our own. That was what was to be seen in the snack bar this morning. We've won admission without honored names to a hard-to-get-into place. Speak bluntly: we want to ask, Is David our peer? There's simply no matching the egalitarianism inside the compound. And I admit I can be exhilarated by it—until the exclusionary obverse obtrudes. Then you're back at the famous phrase: "shut it to open it," etc., wondering who among all of us who say this slogan has an idea what the words might mean.

*

News: what Leo worried about seems to be happening: the energy level is down. He was right, on the face of it, about "comprehensiveness"—at the start it wasn't simply a togetherness of young radicals and old, on the coalition—Rads, Afros, class treasurer, Rhodes Scholar District runner-up, George Kateb our galvanizer, a conservative anti-drug dean, a young faculty activist, a self-proclaimed Marxist aged 42, an eccentric, a golfer, me . . . The student body voted, by an eight-to-one margin, ninety percent of the campus voting, in favor of the first steps toward politicization. More important, it created the first functioning representative student government in years—for the purpose of taking the vote. Supportive faculty resolutions went through unanimously. There were those (not at first ambiguous) gestures of the President's—"implore you to consider"—"deeply sympathetic" —"strong misgivings" . . . An alumni council group spoke out for "interpenetration," seminars with students and faculty, opportunities for public service in the professions", widen them, put the pressure on, open it up, things have got to change . . . The Treasurer of the College himself moved, writing the Trustees to hail a vital new revolution in capitalism on the way, ecology, quality of life, etc. . . . . "Right on"—"sweep of sentiment"—rapping, editing, consulting, doorbelling, advising, arguing, haranguing, inspiring . . .

—But it is mid-May: the students *are* going to clear out, they know it and we can feel it. It's a stronger thing every day at the Committee sessions. We're now highly conscious of being part of a "Coalition," a group that couldn't as individuals be expected to see general experience in the same terms. What a world: I'm "nostalgic" for ten days ago! For a while everybody was experiencing—not just the euphoria of generating "hot events"—but an extreme condition of self-endorsement, moral beatitude. I can live with them! I can *stand* the Enemy at close range (beards, up-tights, SDS bullies, pedant-pigs, black militants, what have you). There's jocularity, camaraderie, even trust in the Committee room. The talk is "one to one." People are "great," they "relate to each other," etc. But cracks appear, people make waves.

Example: I asked about money, used the phrase "keeping track of expenditures." Is there a control on the long distance telephone bill? It's not everyman for himself, is it? The Strike Committee radicals looked sheepish—here was a missed detail. For a second the revolutionary backwound into a boy with an allowance problem—or with a new driver's license and a small dent in Dad's fender . . . After the grin, though, he stiffened, dug in. We need to stay in contact with other schools. How's anybody to know what's happening? The press can't keep tabs on all the schools. They wouldn't want to, couldn't be trusted to. Suppose there are kids in jail, the FBI rigs things, what then? How can you help if nobody knows?

Touching the edge of defiance, I slid off. I hated what I'd for no clear reason become: the accountant. What is this tic in me? I turned to a colleague with a joke about huge phone bills— daughter out of college, still no sense of time . . . Laughter, pledges of stricter control, the meeting moves on. I sit somewhat suppressed, half-embarrassed, half-righteous. Doesn't somebody have to speak about picking up the pieces? . . . I'm exhausted . . . Later at Strike HQ, through an open door, student voices descant on faculty uptightness: ". . . so cheap . . . fantastic!" My face burns as I go by.

But there've been all sorts of rupture: the radicals repeatedly are overzealous in attempting to represent student opinion.

They've been pressing for the fall electioneering recess—but the question is, whom do they speak for? The first campus-wide vote was eight to one—but what would it be now on a new issue? Ans.: consult the Student Assembly. Ah but it's midnight. The condition under which the Student Assembly came into existence was that no action would be taken in its name without a yes or no vote by the full membership. No minority takeovers. And you can't assemble the whole body at this hour— But still the student opinion question has come up and the rads are resourceful. One man leaves the meeting for a quarter of an hour—summons aid, a swift progress from dorm group to dorm group, a "petition" is presented "on behalf of" us, the Steering Committee, the Coalition. Signatures are "amassed." At 2 AM the phone rings—an apologetic moderate, I can't remember his face . . . Do I know that petition-signing is going on? Student Assembly hasn't had a chance to vote yes or no, they're merely being presented with a petition, the signatures will be counted. The rads will imply that, well, if everybody could have been reached, everybody would have signed, a thousand signatures. It's not true. "Sir, can't you stop the signatures from going to the faculty meeting? It'll kill Student Assembly!" . . . In the morning the Coalition centrists—all the phrase means is we want to keep alive a representative faculty-student force capable of challenging the hitherto unchallengeable administrative hegemony—or all it means is some people feeling heavy, slightly depressed, slightly self-important, regretful, stern—we raise the issue. Should the rads have circulated a petition? weren't they breaking a contract? And at that moment the "centrist faction" knows itself as "we," a faction, a moral custodian, the group that talks about obligation, constitutional guarantees, pledges . . . They're the ones that give you "this legalistic bullshit while Hampton gets it up the ass" . . .

Or there's a "problem" with the blacks. Even at the summit of "comprehensiveness" we couldn't hide this one. The instrument creating the Coalition calls for six student members, three from Afro-Am. Afro-Am sends six, announcing that each will have one half of a vote. I laughed too and kept silent and felt my silence as cowardice. Quickly thereafter the attendance of the six declines. We the elders express concern, knowing the Coalition's ongoing credibility requires penetration of the Black Culture Cen-

ter. I feel I'm in the President's shoes, scratching for a "unity."
Any price. We pass the Word. Get the blacks back, can't you
speak to them, get over and talk to them at the Center, we've
got to have them. —We-You-They, a division of role, of sense of
self. The students come back with answers that are curt and
ugly. The blacks say the meetings are too early in the morning,
they're not up. The blacks say the meetings are bullshit. The
blacks say they're working in Springfield, New Haven and New-
ark for and with their own people. The blacks say they'll be
around soon—and in fact they do come around finally—to collect
funds. ("For the above activities the Brothers need much
money," says their mimeo announcement. "It would indeed be
Right on . . . Drop it off in our buckets in the Dining Complex.")
They're resented for this. But mainly I feel self-contempt. I let
this go, and it's part of my "belief system" that this kind of situation must *not* be let go. It's been terribly handled. We could
have gone to them ourselves—the faculty members. We had
capital. There was still some humor around . . . The blacks are
now "over there," the Elders are here, the white rads at the other
table—a room full of betweens . . . Men standing away from each
other, widening the gaps . . .

The key assumption of many of these lads is that the focus
ought to be nothing other than maintaining "spontaneity." (Men
"open up institutions" in order to change the color of the air, end
deadly routine, invent lives that are fun-filled, unexpected,
charming, free; Marcuse in the background, Jerry Rubin up front
—Fred Meyer, a senior, talking for both. An intelligent student.
The goal-oriented, traditional liberal among us doesn't like the
drill. I myself have some sympathy but not an endless amount.
I see that this hostility to the programmatic is somewhat like my
own response to reports of "progress" about dietary deficiencies
in grade school kids in the Delta Counties. The calm, beamishly
offered "statistics"—proof that Planning Can Solve It—make hate
rise in the throat. But still: spontaneity doesn't speak to that. Is it
not—this new watchword—plain self-indulgence? No higher good
than recreation? Schoolchildren seeking a way to shed the upper-
middle-class, fleece-lined hairshirt of boredom—their version of
the Plimpton family's thing—should they be taken seriously?
Isn't their problem lack of acquaintance with true torment? Look

beyond this hour, tomorrow will exist. Forge an instrument, a responsible faculty-student counterforce to the official hierarchy —none's ever existed in the College—a means of working toward significant local change. "The idea isn't schedule-freaking for kicks. 'Opening it up' *means* something—thinking hard, thinking freshly about losses and gains, how to preserve intellectual edge while you try to make it new, aware, *comprehending* . . ."

But the "idea" hasn't been expressed—no time for it. And suspicion of the programmatic is mounting fast. Chatter about bills . . . ballots . . . symbolic blacks. Uptight Responsibility and Efficiency (in my person among others) preening themselves as models for the "spoiled" young—a long way back from here to one-to-oneness. The door opened on togetherness, God save the word, there for a minute—when was it? two weeks ago? . . . How much time is left?

*

Fading faster. This morning was a blow. It was George Kateb again, but not lifting us now, taking us down. Who can speak of "blame"? George told us two weeks ago one justification only could be offered for politicizing the College: the threat to constitutional rights. But each to his own justification. He wanted to purify the campus, empty it of mess, muddle, conflicting aims, erase from mind all Jerry Rubinical slogans ("If there had been no Vietnam War, we'd have invented one"). He constructed the College as a society unified on a little hill of "political morality," in concern for a serious "academic" issue—the threat to reserved rights. Our reserved rights. I can't explain this simply to Benjy . . . I talk about the "over-abstract" quality of George's cause but I don't get through. I wasn't there because of the faculty meeting and I'm just hearing now that, minutes after George spoke at that first rally ages ago, an Afro-Am got up to dispute his claim that the College should be a haven. "Why else are blacks in the jam we're in?"—so said C. P. Ward. It was in the newspaper: no word from Benjy about that. And there was LeRoy after the Commager-Marx session. And there's been no moment in faculty meeting, in workshops, Steering Committee sessions, when "purification" really looked like a live possibility. Each day a new theme, a new injustice wants time on the calendar, a faculty position, recommendations, appropriations. Certain teachers aren't dealing fairly with options concerning grades—pass, fail, incomplete. Fix this, Coalition. A scheduling conflict crosses up Cambodia canvassing with the Panther minister of information's talk. Fix this, Coalition. Buildings and Grounds isn't allowing people time off to participate in Workshops—shouldn't the Coalition "confront" the College Treasurer? Students working on "implications of the Strike for future College Governance" want funds for a survey . . . On the stick, Coalition.

And now this morning we come unstuck. George is in personal anguish. His father is mortally ill in a New York hospital. How can he stand all this? I believe he's also shaken—I know it doesn't have the same weight but it has some—by uncertainty about the constitutional crisis he discerned. (A senior departmental colleague laid out a view opposite to his in faculty meeting. An American historian did the same at College Assembly.) Glum, alert, he's sat through endless sessions of negotiation over what, to his mind, can't seem better than a dungpile of triviality —and now this morning . . . Three college girls claimed time for Women's Lib, "demanded" that we put the case for coeducation to the faculty as a whole. (Some girls on one-year leaves from their own colleges want to stay on here.) We *must* speak out. A girl called Wendy—the world-familiar costume, long straight brown hair, middle part, bell jeans, suspicious eyes—was barely into her discussion when all at once George was shouting. "Take your disgusting pitiable complaints and whining— Take them out! We are talking about dying people, suffering people. There are mothers being burned, children. There's a constitutional crisis! I consider it disgusting that you equate your piddling provocations with this! You should leave!"

The child's mouth was wide. She sat rooted, speechless. Two male students, radical caucus members, were on their feet—a walkout. The door slammed behind them. George sat trembling. The student chairman blinked and blinked again. Someone asked the stunned girl a question and George rose, excused himself, left us. Does it matter what I "felt"? Foolish, incompetent, ridden with sympathies, leaf in the rapids . . . I sat half-grinning, wanting to apologize to the world. Nobody *clarifies*—my usual thought,

my permanent thought. Coeducation now isn't coeducation then,
girls and boys—relations among them—it's all different! . . . It all
has to be explained, articulated. Can't do it in a minute, a day . . .

And then there's George's "situation." A purifier, he'd conceived an abstract political world—is this what the university is
for, to enable a mind so to imagine? He'd conceived something
abstract and, enclosed within it—a world of political talk about
political talk like that imagined in Hannah Arendt's treatise "On
Revolution"—he'd found it possible to imagine a college "properly" committed to politics. But the forces unleashed by his imagination, the inconceivable mix of issues, the rush of difficult
strangers—Panthers, Fem Libs, workers, supers—drove down on
him, preyed on his grief, swept him out of the room.

—You could put it this way: before we managed even to begin to talk we looked around and saw we were right at the edge
of a cliff. After that it was all worry about hanging on.

✳

Home from a sour faculty meeting. Ugly tempers. Cynicism.
Someone stood up to berate students for a piece of bad manners
remembered from the previous week, and—to his own evident
surprise—found himself applauded, cheered . . . two votes were
taken almost without debate on proposals for electioneering recesses for the fall—overwhelming defeats . . . an economist told
a joke, smiling as he spoke— If there's going to be any of this
fiddling with vacations, the thing to do is not mess around with
Thanksgiving but just start earlier and end earlier. "Every year
we have these troubles, every year we have them in the spring.
The minute warm weather comes all hell breaks loose. I say get
'em out of here earlier—" Laughter, applause, laughter . . . "Is
that a motion?" "No, just the truth . . ." Laughter, laughter, applause . . .

Not a single voice speaking from the unity, the "comprehensiveness," the sense of possibility. Why so? Ans.: "They" are going
home. That pushing, prodding crowd . . . They waited outside,
mostly, but once three of them came in uninvited, forcing an ad-
journment . . . When they're here, the students, the faculty
majority is cautious, formal, fact-findingly neutral—when they're

here. When it's time for them to leave—they've actually hung on much longer than anyone thought they could—the signal is passed: OK, you can come out now, chaps, *relax* . . .

Bitterness? A little . . . But again the "personal" enters—cheer comes with it this time. Benjy eavesdropped on the first page or two of my commencement talk—all I have—and passed judgment at supper. —What's that on your desk? Answer: I have to write a talk. . . . Well, don't just sit there. Did you like it? Answer: It's good. I liked it a lot. . . . So, if we get through to the end, I'll bring Benjy along to Pa. and have a family ovation after all . . . My irremediably trivializing reductive self . . .

*

An unexpected visitor just now: Cal Plimpton, calling to say he's resigning, will stay on a year as a lame duck. He promised the Trustees to stay ten years, he's completed his term, we're ready for a fresh start. . . . He wouldn't have quit as long as there was danger of an explosion, stick with the ship, of course. But we're in shoal waters now, we've made it. . . . It's not a personal call. The President wants his Planning Committee to go on working, lay on something helpful for the new president. . . . I'm one of the faculty planners—the Long Rangers, as the local wits tease us. Cal and I have an awkward drink and my feeling goes out to him. Surely he would have wanted to stay in office a little longer. When exactly was the moment of crisis for him? The moment of decision. . . . Weigh his faults, yes, but is there a chance we can do better?

It's the kind of event, as it turns out, that induces river-of-life thoughts. I hardly think of him, I think of me. He arrived my first year as a full professor. I've therefore seen him "come and go." I remember when he first entered a faculty meeting. He waited at the front of the room, unselfconsciously, until introduced by his own lame duck predecessor and then rose and spoke softly, peffickly for perfectly, here a Boston bit, there some Midatlantica. (The accent was familar because it resembled his half brother's —F. T. P. Plimpton, a senior trustee.) He was very grateful, he said, for this chance to meet with the faculty and share his thoughts, as he hoped we would share our thoughts in time with him. He hoped some of us might write a letter telling of our personal interests and hopes for the College. We could become acquainted in this way. His own interest, he went on, had been in the behavior of men facing the situation of being ill, even mortally ill. Their way of thinking and talking and journeying with you. —The man speaking was exceptionally tall, hunched over from probably 6' 5"—black suit, white shirt, regimental stripe, black hair close-cropped—black loafers! The voice was pleasant, uninflected, seemingly utterly undesirous of calling attention by emphases or dynamics to a line of argument. There was no argument. The President-elect was not saying, You know about your things, I know about mine, possibly these two kinds of knowledge can swap back and forth in the barrel and improve each other. He simply had launched on a short talk about ill people in hospitals, remarking that he was impressed by their courage, impressed by the way people could sometimes bear with you and trust you when they were hopelessly alone, impressed by their power to rise to a certain height and face what lay before them with great calm. There were few connectives in the talk—or in any talk subsequently given by the President. No therefores, no buts, no concessive clauses. "Although some say this, I say that—" —not a hint of subordination or other rhetoric of persuasion. The voice flowed on and listeners had the sense that, if logical connections were weak, substantive matters, unusual matters, had nevertheless been placed before them. A meditative man? A contemplative—nothing willful, contentious, disputative. "It will be interesting," said the Chairman of the English Department thoughtfully at a meeting that afternoon. "He's seen men die." The first clear impression was of a person of privilege, remote from common areas of academic opinionation, undemanding, indisposed to contention—interesting, possibly irrelevant.

Did not the loafers count? Perhaps. There are moments when the President's face tells not only of high sophistication, but also about humor and inner resource—a fully civilized face, round, faintly puffy at the cheekbones, elegance in the hair line, a self-mocking, waiting look about the mouth, combining the disposition to tease with a boyish air of being caught with hand in jam jar. Nobody could dislike him; he's wholly engaging in manner, attractive, easy, no hint of a taut cord anywhere in his being.

Yet the hunched shoulders, the black suits, the immense arms, the peculiar huddled-rolling-ground-engulfing gait, give the impression, especially from behind, of a kind of clerical King Kong— a lusus naturae, a strange object. And the man seems to have a sense of this. You almost think he feels his height as a wound: he never imposes it. He has no vanity, no self-regard, communicates good-humored awareness of his size as deformity. He's not clumsy but there's something that suggests he thinks clumsiness is, in his case, imminent, terribly hard to avoid. In other words: he treats himself as a vulnerable comic figure, a person nobody in his right mind could be afraid of.

Probably that was why he succeeded as he succeeded? No one quite took in the fundamental seriousness. —Is it right to talk of "success"?

Of course there's the matter of the name, and the circumstances of the original appointment. In the contest between the pride of the aristocrat and the pride of the self-made there's no sure winner—but there's a contest, oh my yes. Uncelebrated faculty stood in the same relation to the President as that between obscure students and David Eisenhower, and we weren't any more disposed to defer. Cataloguing the Plimptonian "advantages," riffling through the cloud of silky identifying labels—Harvard, Riverdale, Piping Rock, West Hills, Exeter, Rosemary Hall, Osterville, Wiano, Mill Reef, Brook, River—these aren't nightly recreations. But which of us didn't know this was a family that allowed none of its brood to sink, that sought not subsistence but an "interesting life," that didn't earn its way in the conventional manner? Possibly they themselves had an illusion or two on that point—here is my egalitarianism. Francis Taylor Pearsons Plimpton, the elder brother, could remark that his son George had "made an interesting life for himself," as though assured the life was truly self-made. He could also come before a faculty committee (years ago) and ask blandly, no mention of his brother as the candidate his fellow trustees had in mind, how the faculty would feel about a "medical doctor"—as though his brother's being a doctor would determine how we felt, not his brother's being his brother. The illusions probably intensified our skepticism . . . Some of the meaner jokes about privilege made about Cal Plimpton's appointment still haven't been forgotten. (It was

said that the family, having provided the young nephew with
the Yankees, the Lions, the NY Philharmonic as toys, felt something should be done for the uncle—so they'd bought him a college to amuse him.)

The notion implicit in the jokes, that the Plimptons were
dilettantes among serious men, wasn't fair. Ambitious public men
have taken them seriously. Several of the family have worked to
significant public effect in recent days, have tasted the arena,
know the feeling of having touched a hot center, felt close to
power. George Plimpton and his young bride were movers in the
Bobby Kennedy effort in New York. Francis Plimpton was pivotal
in the defeat of Haynesworth-Carswell. The President himself,
decorated for helping in the Lebanon troop landing, has cards
of entry to Arab circles closed to American diplomats and private
citizens and he is used. But all this rarely figures locally, when
we think about him. The habit is to smile, to "enjoy" him, to
treat him lightly, accept him as likable, good-natured, "human,"
soft, uncommitted in intellectual matters, a man in loafers, jolly,
pliant, playful, uncomfortable in argument, "goes along easily . . ."

What would have been required to alter that understanding,
to intimate to us sooner that behind these shadows stood something iron? Was it iron? Would it have helped if, on formal occasions—convocation, graduation and the like—his manner had
shifted a little, had grown in sharpness of definition? Maybe. At
moments of pomp the same man appeared—in the loafers—showing an intensely likable embarrassment with the position of sole
speaker, commander, conductor. The President hurried his public
words, sloughing over points of emphasis. He read invariably as
though from an address unfamiliar to him, a speech written by
another man (he wrote his own stuff) who unfortunately had
been taken ill, could not appear, sent his paper on in his place.
He was heard by us as a man who could not believe in the substantial reality of his place, who had not fully come into phase
with robes and authority and office, who felt within himself—
rightly?—that it was a kind of odd humorous accident he was
there before "us," in much the way it was odd that he was anywhere—for quickly enough (mobility on his order being what it
was) he'd be somewhere else. It was always impossible to imagine him as having driven toward this place, of having gathered

himself in successive objective competitions against other candidates, pointing himself thitherward . . . He was necessarily seen as having dropped down, at the cost (to him) of perpetual unseriousness, remoteness from personal commitment . . .

Who could treat at his proper worth a leader who often treated himself as a joke? Who could believe in him as the key opponent to a committed majority of any kind! How unlikely that his decisions and actions could shape the whole life of a significant academic institution! He was a "cooperator." Nobody ever stamped feet for President Plimpton in Chapel. A "marshmallow," said a senior faculty member early in the reign: doesn't have an edge. —It's these old families, said someone else: reread Henry Adams. —Not serious, said still another voice: doesn't care about the issues.

What was wrong with us? Here was someone possessing the normal skills of the class—club doubles, sailing, mountain-climbing (the Matterhorn, natch), squash, pool, etc. Here was good competence at languages (serviceable French, Spanish, German and Arabic) and musical performance (spirited fourhanded piano). The President taught Zen and poetry in a fraternity house, met regularly with his Chaucer group in New York, taught in the basic natural science course at the College, whenever the labs took a bio-chem turn, was curator of a family collection of paintings of the English poets and knew the lives through the portraits in a serious caring way.

Nor was he merely an "accomplished" man. He'd held teaching and administrative posts at the College of Physicians and Surgeons. He's on the Harvard Board of Overseers—Trustee of Exeter—Trustee at U. Mass-Boston, a committeeman at the Amercan Council on Education. He raised $20 million in two years without becoming an absentee president, chairing all faculty meetings (in his manner), interviewing all job candidates (in his manner), introducing qualities of social openness to the President's house which, in the opinion of oldtimers (I don't quite qualify), hadn't been known in that place in all its previous history. Men who caught side glances of him were eager to talk of his energy—campus cops saw him at his desk regularly at dawn . . . Milt Smith the College Chauffeur reported that he never simply sits, that he dictates, reads, writes constantly on his airport trips. Late at night he might doze, coming in at 2 or 3 AM, a messed-up flight—but he'd be in the office early. "The way you could tell he's tired," said Milt. "He almost always knows the minute I turn up the hill he's home—he's awake sitting up in back. The way you know he's had it is when I pull up in front of the house and he's still asleep in the back and I have to say, Cal? Cal? It doesn't happen too often but it happens. I don't know how he stands it."

Not even a college presidency could put an end to the doctoring: he made housecalls in the town throughout his term. He was, according to his joke, at the bottom of a long local list. "When they get down to the chiro and he's out and the vet's away and there's no raising the Christian Science practitioner, there's still old Plimpton, might as well call him." As far as can be made out, no member of the faculty, no faculty wife, and few members of the student body went to the hospital with a serious ailment, during the sixties, without hearing from their own physician that "your leader" had made a call of inquiry and concern. The campus cop with a bleeding ulcer was watched over with the rest. Norman Birnbaum in Sociology, so excruciated he couldn't sit down in faculty meetings, had to stand up for hours in the rear of the room, a terrible pain in his back—no help from anyone in the Valley . . . The President helped him, gave him a New York doctor, an idea what the trouble might be—and he was right . . . An operation, benign tumor . . . Norman's eyes moisten when he tells you, My God what a diagnostician . . . The thirteenth President of Amherst College pushed himself hard, chaps—near-Kennedy levels of intensity. A deep sense of obligation to others . . . The idea of him as soft, undriven, ineffectual—

—Listen, you thought we had problems with the man: without him we could have agony.

●

The Commencement issue of the paper. Fred Meyer explains, in a forgiving tone, why the Strike collapsed. I sit out in the sun reading it and feel bloody. The author sat beside us, worked with us, "rapped," shared the jokes, the attempt at purposefulness. He remembers the high days, all right: "There was a sense of unity

. . . There was a sense of what could be accomplished, a bursting forth from the shell we had been set in. Out of sight, out of mind . . . The spontaneity was simply astounding . . ." But he remembers it as existing *before* us. *We* ruined it. He forgives us, but it was our fault. "We" being the old boys . . . "The spontaneity was simply astounding . . . Nobody was sleeping, calls were coming in from all over the country about strikes . . . [We] were an organic body with no real hierarchy. Decisions were made on the spot. Individuals gravitated to those activities that needed manpower . . . [We] were getting in touch with local schools, prep schools, high schools, for workshops, talks, etc. by faculty and students . . . Students and faculty were able to talk to each other in a new way . . ." But then came: "The Student-Faculty Steering Committee (basically a line of communication and organization), [and] the spontaneity was over . . . The form which the Amherst strike found for itself inevitably led to the inertia I see around me and in myself, the depression we are feeling, that we are going nowhere . . . The Strike staggered to a halt, not knowing where to go, coopted in a sense by well-meaning and over-organized liberals."

What was the key moment? Fred believes it was Women's Lib:

> By . . . Sunday when the Women's Liberation group came to talk to the Student-Faculty Steering Committee . . . the Amherst strike had set its goals, which did not include, perhaps rightly for the moment, coeducation. The meeting was not pleasant. The real struggle was between liberal and radical factions, just as it was to be at the National meeting in New Haven on Wednesday, May 14. For tactical reasons (i.e. not to offend) many wanted to address only the war issue . . . a fundamental error in analysis, etc. etc.

I move on to the gym, procession forming. The word here is that the Alumni Fund is off—a bad blow, $60,000 down, 500 fewer contributors. "Never happened before," the Alumni man insists. The news draws us together. Feeling is flowing for Cal Plimpton. How he'll be missed . . . Everyone's tone is conciliatory—even I. F. Stone cottons up to the Moms and Dads, speaks for them. Kids mustn't be too hard on America . . .

The President acts stern, as though (for a minute) he's not

in the market for friends. The Charge to the Seniors lays him out in full view almost for the first time. He discloses in his talk that he considers the student hubbub about injustice to be traceable to affluence on the one hand, and arrogance on the other. He acknowledges (by implication) that he signed the moratorium letter to the White House only because it was a way of keeping the peace—not because the thing expressed his views. In his opinion, faculty members—the people he made common cause with yesterday, "imploring" the head of state, and against whom he took no stand while the students were around in numbers— faculty members lack self-control in time of pressure. From the first he had bent mind and will fully to the work of preventing the institution from being shut down in the name of any cause— "openness," peace or whatever. And no strategy or tactic of his aimed toward that end was vulnerable to any responsible charge of impropriety.

Listening, it's easy for me to remember the provocations, the temptations to draw a line—everything he'd resisted in the past. The severe presidential self-denials, presidential self-discipline. He acted at all hours of confrontation and challenge in the name of his great cause: abolition of difference, preservation of what is. When, at times of serious exacerbation, he was forced to acknowledge "difference"—between himself and a thin faculty majority, he adopted, in a putative manner, the majority sentiment, thus closing the threatened gap. Nothing surprising in any of this—it was perfectly evident. But to acknowledge it virtually in so many words! To acknowledge it only when the majority of the dissidents had left the campus, leaving behind a tiny band of "militants" whose energies had long before been sapped!

I sat remembering his provocations, trying to swing with the Great Reconciliation. The famous moratorium faculty meeting. The dean read aloud the letter Leo Marx had proposed—the letter the President had to sign—and what was it like then? . . . In the science lecture hall, they were down in the well. The Dean read the thing slowly, with emphasis, and with us looking down from above. The President sat desultorily, long limbs stretched beneath a table—was it vacancy or embarrassed boredom or what? I remember how he looked. What a humiliation for the man! People stood around afterward saying that. I remember it clearly.

". . . I felt sorry for Cal sitting there . . ." After all, the proposal of a letter to Nixon should, by protocol, first have been addressed privately to President Calvin Plimpton, the official college spokesman, providing him with an opportunity to weigh his response unsandbagged. But as it was . . . half the room listened to the Dean's reading, half looked at the President looking at his hands. Hardly a word of the text bore his stamp, reflected his mode of address to life. Hardly one word recognizably his own. What self-respecting man could have seen himself at this moment—a college president hearing words written for him, as though he were a mute—words to be passed off publicly to others as his own—who could have faced such a situation without anger, a sense of being used, dispossessed?

On the final phrases the Dean paused—then added: —"signed, Calvin Plimpton." Applause burst on the room, the faculty on its feet. The President ducked in his chin as though avoiding a shot, grinned, looked up at the Dean, up at the blaring, cheering rows. He was still seated. He grinned sheepishly, moved his hand as though in a you-first movement to point to Leo, to acknowledge that this was not his applause, his letter. —Hard to forget that! The applause went on. The faculty was applauding itself, applauding the conception of the letter, applauding the idea of its own necessary emergence—symbolically "above" the President— and different from him—as the dominant force on the campus. —Sorry, "Cal," regrets at interrupting the jolly, ten-year, Great Funfest. But there are times when *serious* men must assert themselves, and such an hour's at hand. . . .

No intensity of application is required to place in view the probable human responses at this moment. No honorable man can feel at one with himself when he knows that applause directed at him isn't for him, or he knows that praise accorded him is meant for another man in the same room. The impulse to break out toward open acknowledgment—concession of difference— would ride down most proud or self-willed men. It would surely have been intensified by public congratulations, from newspapers, other college administrators, government officials. (There was a lot of that and it's still coming. On June 16, 1970, the *Times* lead editorial began: "More than a year ago, President Calvin H. Plimpton of Amherst College warned President Nixon that, while there is no magic formula for campus peace, there is no hope for a moderate consensus so long as many students feel that 'the nation has no adequate plans for meeting the crises of our society.'") Whence comes the power to bear the glance of those who think you're a fraud, a counterfeit, a receiver of stolen praise? From the gut. From certainty about who you are, what you believe, what you understand your job to be. The President's job was to facilitate the flow of harmless protest, to permit the community to see itself as acting fearlessly, responsibly, and imaginatively for the public good, to provide a circumstance in which men could freshly discover the joy of freedom of utterance with the thrill of risk—his job was to do these things at whatever cost to self, for the purpose of maintaining the unity of the institution and insuring the continued powerlessness of the dissidents.

Was the institution harmed (from the Establishment point of view) by this self-righteous letter? Less than it would have been by a President who insisted on pointing out that some in the community could not accept such a document as expressive of their views. Was the institution harmed, six months later, when, after another suspension of classes forced by a building-takeover, black students crowded the aisles in a mass meeting at the Chapel —voices interrupting, shouts of Bullshit!—vapid cries of "Power to the People"? Less than it might have been by a demand for decorum. Was the institution harmed in February when, at another mass meeting, a Smith girl shrilled that: "We don't trust you, President Plimpton, we don't trust you."? Less than it might have been had the President chosen to confront the abusive remarks. At the confrontation with the blacks, the President "didn't hear" the mutterings against him; he offered the platform to the blacks and then to Leo Marx, as leading radical faculty spokesman. At the Committee confrontation, he met the fierce charge and fierce Fem Lib face (the girl's name was Joan Annett) with a steady sorrowful glance, and the words, "I know that, Miss Annett. I know that," thereafter turning away to take another question, and another, for three hours.

Was it not duplicitous?—back comes the question. Wasn't it wrong so to control and hide your response to provocation, so to imply by silence that you might assent to charges made against you? Not, maybe, if you knew where you were going, that in the end your chance to say your own piece, recover your dignity—and in the process Bring Them All Together Again—would arrive. And it had indeed arrived. The game was the same. Overtly Cal Plimpton chided us, accused us of panic, showed us he'd never "agreed," never been "of our faction." But the ground note wasn't accusatory: he confessed "our" misdeeds as though they were his. There couldn't have been any air of chicanery, for him, hanging round the words. He once again embraced the whole with a pronoun, recreated the "saving oneness" nearly lost. The delivery of the Charge to the Seniors was maybe a shade different from earlier presidential speechifying—slightly more deliberately-paced, clearer, stronger in movement. The newspaper "reviews" were as before: meaning, the *Times* was as positive about these words that were truly the President's as it had been a year before about words of opposite import and different authorship. ("Eloquent" was the paper's word.) "In the past thirteen months," the President confessed for all present:

> . . . we have allowed, and even aided and abetted, the near closing of this College on three separate occasions. Our disapproval of events in Cambodia and racism have led us to strike at the nearest and flimsiest of all institutions, a college. No matter where the blow was aimed, it struck the College . . . In moments of crisis we have panicked and been shocked lest there be business 'as usual'—knowing all the while that crises are the very moments when usual and normal procedures are most valuable and necessary. There is an old saying that a man will bleed to death in three minutes from a severed carotid artery, but a surgeon can suture it in two minutes if he isn't hurried by panic . . . We have tried to throw away what we now have, however imperfect it may be, simply to express our outrage at what is happening elsewhere. It reminds me slightly of that grim Israeli story of the man who murders his father and then seeks compensation as an orphan! Add to this the general distrust which students, professors, and institutions have aroused, compound this with the general distrust which students and professors have of educational institutions in particular, and society as a whole, and it is indeed incredibly difficult to define one's relationship to a particular college . . .

—Incredibly difficult, and yet possible, if men would but give over their fantasies of dispute, their wars of words, their self-enclosed worlds of opinionation, their vanities . . . The President's voice ran on, teasing, gentling the departing students out of their edginess, calling forth from parents, babes in arms, the county sheriff, the voice of the Commonwealth, the kindly "Izzy" Stone in an orange shirt—calling forth from all an admission of the uselessness of separating yourself from your brother. Within the enclave, a large future ahead, openings everywhere—what was the point, now, really, of this "protest thing"? Dust rose, dust fell in the gray morning light of the Cage. Some memory of a voice came back into my head, a long return, talking of a journey, the courage to trust in someone else when there is nothing— no hope left, only courage. And then men were on their feet shouting, applauding. Eustace Seligman, the senior emeritus trustee, was prodding at somebody on the center platfrom—a professor of Romance Languages—who wasn't on his feet. "—you got up for him [I. F. Stone], get up, you got up for *him*" . . . People are turning to each other, looking out at the students, they're standing and applauding . . . Strike's over. We still have the right to say "we."

✿

Tonight, avoiding finishing my talk—it's the day after tomorrow, and who won't be sick of words by then, *everywhere?*— I brood on two passages from Ortega, found in Auden's Commonplace book:

> The young man plays at busying himself with problems of the collective type, and at times with such passion and heroism that anyone ignorant of the secrets of human life would be led to believe that his preoccupation was genuine. But, in truth, all this is a pretext for concerning himself with himself, and so that he may be occupied with self.

And:

> During periods of crisis, positions which are false or feigned are very common. Entire generations falsify themselves to themselves; that is to say, they wrap themselves up in artistic styles, in doctrines, in political movements which are insincere and which fill

the lack of genuine conviction. When they get to be about forty years old, those generations become null and void, because at that age one can no longer live on fictions.

—Well what is it, "young" man: are you living on fictions? Are you merely preoccupied with self? . . .

❀

My commencement talk began with an incident, almost as though I was determined at any cost not to lose touch with particulars:

I'll start if I may with a moment, not dramatic or overwhelming. I'm in Mississippi, about to engage in summertime good works. With a group of students from my college and Smith college, I'm there to help in a tutorial program for black youngsters who're entering integrated schools for the first time in the fall. It's evening. The singing of hymns and protest songs on the lawn is finished, the kids are in their rooms studying opening-day assignments or larking about—awful truants they are already—with their tutors. I'm hot and thirsty. Too much travel. Too many fancy briefings. My bunkmate in our trailer house—I've just arrived but he's been here for a week—says we need beer. We take the project station wagon, drive down the hill, across the highway into town. The name is West Point, and you reach this town, traveling southeast from Memphis, on a highway whose signs and markers resound in the memory—scenes of racial atrocities read about over the years. Read about in the cosy comfort of winter mornings in a study before class, at leisure, fire going—front page bottom box of the *New York Times*—Greenwood, Grenada, Mc-Comb . . .

I see beer signs on the way but, says my bunkmate, we don't hack around there. I understand, naturally. As Yankee visitors, we're not well-regarded by local people, and anyway going to Blacktown is a gesture of solidarity with the people we're trying to help. Who needs this explained? . . .

We turn in from a paved road to a dirt one, slatternly one-story frame buildings, stores, tin roofs extended over the walks—a gallery effect, sort of. We slip up to the curb, diagonal parking. A black man and woman—his wife?—a woman with a baby in her arms—they're standing outside the beer parlor. No, they're looking in the window—they're watching the TV inside. Not there for beer, just for the program, baby awake for a bit. They're pretty involved in the show. I wait a half-second, smiling at storefront communal TV. I climb out, shut the door. The sound surprises them. The black man looks at me. Instantly he steps off the walk into the gutter, pulling the woman's elbow. She's with him. —This way of talking about it doesn't communicate the fact. It splits the act up as though there were stages or a moment of choice or decision but no, there wasn't any. This was a single moment of human response or recognition—the black man turns, sees us, moves himself and his wife and child from our path, though they are not *in* our path. They don't look up. I feel locked into the deed of moving past them. I'd like to say something. Well look . . . I'm from out of town, it's your town, it's your *section*. You shouldn't—You shouldn't move like that. Nothing to be afraid of. They are merely there, waiting for me to go by. It comes out from the man, a strong projecting abasing current, that they have a sense of themselves as trespassers, guilty, dangerously guilty because a white man has parked his car close to them, a strange white advancing past them toward—really past them?—toward the Blacktown beer parlor door. Or does he want their place at the window watching a Carol Burnett summer repeat? No turf on this earth is theirs, they are automatically cowed. They have no right to stand or to look. They can't even inquire—in the honored way people inquire glancingly and deprecatingly about strangers. "Who's that over there? I wonder who that is?" Not for them to know. This elementary primitive freedom—it's not *there*. The child in the mother's arms—could he or she feel the quick movement, the guilty instinctive fearful motion of retreat? Soak it right into the bones before they're old enough to utter a word?

I went on to explain to my audience that I wasn't out to break anybody's heart, that I brought up this memory—a moment of wariness, a mother and father sweeping themselves like dust-puffs out of my path: that really was what it was like—I was bringing it up only because it was the kind of moment that inevitably came to mind when you had to think about such matters as "Scholarship and Social Commitment" (this was the title settled upon six months before). It came to mind because it had registered as pure evil and had had an impact on my "social commitment," and made me question why there wasn't more nourishment for such commitment in the world of scholarship. My idea was, I said, that the impulse to commitment is nourished by "moments of humane impact . . . direct swift sudden graspings of damage done to a fellow human creature by social injustice or meanness. Moments that blot out the time and circumstances around them and make us understand from inside some commonplace routinized reduction or wounding of human-ness, some habitual deprivation of pride that hitherto we knew only as words."

I tried then to explain why such moments were rare in academic life. I talked a little, deprecatingly, patronizingly, uneasily, about the "seductive clubbiness" of the world of scholarship—"one more white middle-class enclave providing most who enter with an uncommon sense of solidarity with each other and with a thousand ways of assuring themselves that the experience of the people outside is, in some sense at least, represented among them." And, more uneasily, I put in a few licks at "the scholarly habit of mind," on the ground that it "tends to factor out separate moments of response or being into diffuse perspectives, pushing the experience away into the abstraction, so that the integrity of humane impact in this or that moment of revelation can't sustain its original force":

> We know that scholarship enforces a comparative, historical, skeptical mode of response. We know that the scholar's world is a world of relationships, variables—a world in which it's assumed, rightly, that sound knowledge presses its way through any single given situation into the multitude of other situations that somewhere bear on the first, or are comparable to it or are interestingly divergent from it. Sound knowledge breaks open, we say, the isolation chambers of the bleeding heart, leads us out of the cult of self-dramatization or the prison of self-absorption, toward objective comprehension, evaluation, acts of placement. The scholar must seek more than his heart's reasons. He must overgo Self.

> It is a heady command: Overgo Self. It is an invitation to the glory of self-control—hard to resist. Hard not to slip into the comparatistic mode and out of private anguish. The enticement of comprehensiveness has a nearly irresistible power for *any* man capable of thought—and not alone for professors or students.

My audience was with me, I knew this, as I came out of my examples and moved to the end. I hadn't given such a talk before. It wasn't clear to me how the voice (my other voice) that several times weekly invites speculation about the inner life of Masha and Vershinin or Hermione and Leontes (advice to the players) —how it conceivably could become this voice. The man talking, gesticulating, intense, "sincere"—was he also the character who sloped away hours in front of the New Books shelf in the library? received in the mail and read with mild interest Professor T. J. Assad's paper on "Time and Eternity: Tennyson's 'A Farewell' and 'In the Valley of Cauteretz?'" looked forward to an Anglo-American–Dutch conference on popular culture and literary criticism (paper still to write for that) in Holland on Labor Day?

But I didn't lack for confidence. I even ventured to set yesterday's Commencement speaker straight:

> Consider what happened the day before yesterday at my college commencement. The speaker was I. F. Stone, editor of I. F. Stone's *Newsletter*. For years this correspondent has been a brilliant and effective critic of American adventurism in foreign policy. Long before I and others like me knew or cared about the issues he spoke to, he was trying to rouse us. For years he's functioned as a courageous, independent journalist prepared to address the harsh word to immediate situations, and not victimized by Long Views. Once in the academy, however, Mr. Stone did our thing—the thing all of us by training and habit in this environment do: he turned comparatist. He tried to understand everybody. After some criticism of the Cambodian adventure, some mention of the admirable qualities of the young, some teasing of David Eisenhower (who chose not to come, having said he wouldn't, if Mr. Stone was the speaker), and some praise of long hair, Mr. Stone launched an historical account of human turpitude—as a way of counseling young and old against extravagances of protest. After all, said this former voice of protest, after all, racism is everywhere. Look at the Russians and their treatment of the Jews, consider Northern Ireland, consider the tribalism of Nigeria: see the rule of human viciousness everywhere. Think of Milton, read him: think of sin. And as for freedom, and the charges made that our country is turning repressive: well, face it, we are still enormously freer than most of the world. "I can speak against government policy in government buildings in Washington. That's pretty good, isn't it" . . . This is not a Fascist country. . . . Find your balance, Nixon is not Hitler nor was Johnson Hitler. Get a clear perspective, see matters in the round, understand the greatness of what you have, don't risk tearing down what you possess.

> —Is this not plausible talk? Is there not a "lot in it"? Is it not appropriate in tone and in truth to a university setting, to a world of scholars, to an audience of fathers and mothers joyous at the achievements of their sons' and their own hard labor?

All round the room you felt how deeply appropriate it was. All round the room you felt the sense of ease returning. At least he wasn't beating up the daddies and mothers. At least he wasn't saying it was time for revolution. Relief. Thank God. At the end, applause-time, parents stood first, at length a few students, then the whole great Cage. We were brought together, reconciled, made one. It happened several times more that morning. In our state of mind we were somehow even at one with the Panthers— we *forgave* them. Naturally they are extreme, but it is because they don't know what we know, if they but knew that in Hungary or that in Czechoslovakia— Well, I myself thought of items Mr. Stone might have quoted to us. He might have quoted the Polish emigré Leopold Tyrmand declaring that his recently published book was "the first book I could write in complete freedom. American institutions—which are here taken for granted, like oxygen—are the subject of our wildest dreams in Eastern Europe. I have a certain pity for the Americans, because they do not know how to cherish what they have."

What was happening as Mr. Stone spoke was that we were in process of adopting a tone of detachment and understanding at the cost of losing our sense of the moment-to-moment life of people who can't share this tone with us. We were in process of transforming thousands of individual crises of feeling and of protest, millions beyond counting of denials of humanity—moments of being forced to be less than a man, less than a person—we were transforming them into matters of ignorance. We were teaching ourselves that provocation to violence in our society lies not in a specific condition, or in specific terrors or deprivations of men in our midst. We were saying to ourselves, Oh, the cause of our troubles is the widespread ignorance of the relation between these seemingly exacerbating conditions and some others in different ages, different cultures, different places on earth. . . . Would our radical activists really be so upset about policemen shooting blacks in their beds or about black children being spat upon by white teachers or about Indians shuffled from territory to territory by blank bureaucrats, or about Chicanos treated as stupid for "not knowing English" . . . Would they be so upset about this if they knew what's gone on in the past, or what it's like in some of these islands in the Caribbean now, or in mid-nineteenth century Ireland, or South Africa? . . . Well, let us forgive them, let us forgive them all, let us forgive all the extremists—let us only hope for the day when they too will join us in the comparatistic, tolerant, unflappable, tragical-comprehensive view of life.

As I said these words I felt clearminded and strong. I claimed that my purpose wasn't in any sense to mock the university environment:

> My purpose here is only to express once more the familiar fear of scholarship as a force for obliviousness: to express this fear at the risk of being charged with anti-intellectualism, or lack of concern for the human need for models of consecutive thought and coherent use of the mind. My purpose is only to say that at the moment at which our enclave—our white middle-class spaceship called the liberal arts college—touches down once more, triumphantly or otherwise, another voyage done, it is right to forego every gesture of self-satisfaction, every movement of mind that tells us, comparatistically, that "things really aren't so bad as all that." I want to say we need an unmanned father, a spat-upon black child, with us in this room, in the chair beside us. We need this not because we wish voluptuously to savor our guilt but because we should care for true knowledge, whole knowledge: we should wish truly to know how things are, within experienced dailiness, for ourselves and our brothers. If we put ourselves aside, if we open up this room and let them stand near us, the black man, the wife, the child—not particularly moving, simply surprising—or the pusher at noon outside the Sock It To Me Baby candystore on Amsterdam Avenue, if we press to know this experience from within, to live imaginatively into a life composed exclusively of unlucky moments, we may free ourselves from abstraction. And if we don't we will never be educated.

I had no sense of being "in bad faith," of having "sold out," of having lost touch with the values and standards of "the profession." I looked out over the packed gym, over the faculty heads, and ended the thing with a charge:

> Class of '70: you and I need this freedom from abstraction, this penetration of an instant of feeling, if you are going to survive the century and I'm to survive the decade. You and I need a way to stay in touch with the moment of being in which we know at the root of our breathing that society must not be left as it is. You and I need a way to hold fast to an enormously wearing doubleness: that we must not lose what we have, yet must not be content with it. I wish we—colleges and academies in general—could have helped you more. I believe we'll do better for those who come after you, move closer to an experiential edge. I believe it's wholly possible to do better. But while we're waiting, getting ready for the September that's always somehow here in June, even though you leave, what we can do is see the nature of the job—sustaining a doubleness, inspiring both our conserving

and reforming selves, earning the right by the quality of our private daily doings to win general wars against complacencies and privilege, never giving over the hard endless struggle to feel.

It was only at the moment of the "ovation" that I saw myself as a stranger.

❋

In my box this morning the August form letter from the bookshop—they need to order required texts now (English 31, English 69). I've had some ideas, of course, some real enthusiasm, in fact—amidst second thoughts, self-accusation, new intransigence. Am no doubt looking forward. And at my age (in any case) you don't change everything. But it's right to record that I've been extremely slow this time settling definitely on my lists. Partly it's that it's harder than usual to know what's likely to go well, partly it's realizing that definiteness of every kind—of self or of subject—truly is on its way out. Can't wait forever, though—"hanging loose," breathing deep . . . Tomorrow I'll take my plunge.

ACKNOWLEDGMENTS

The author thanks Ralph Beals, Arnold Collery, Margaret DeMott, Jean Dunbar, Mary Heath, George Kateb, Allen Kenyon, Virginia McDermott, Bea McKie, Leo Marx, Marietta Pritchard, William Pritchard and John William Ward for generous help of many kinds.

Benjamin DeMott, author of *Supergrow* and the novel *A Married Man,* lives with his wife and four children (one grown, one in college and two in school) in Amherst, Massachusetts. This is Professor DeMott's twentieth year as an English teacher at Amherst College.

photo by Jim Gerhard

0371

0-525-21310

DATE DUE

JUN 5 '74			
E H			
GAYLORD			PRINTED IN U.S.A.